CURRENT AFRICAN ISSUES 55

Academics on the Move

Mobility and Institutional Change in the Swedish Development Support to Research Capacity Building in Mozambique

Måns Fellesson & Paula Mählck

A case study for the NAI research project:
Academic Mobility in Africa – Modes and Narratives of Mobility and
Institutional Change in International Donor-Supported Programs Targeting
Research Capacity-Building

NORDISKA AFRIKAINSTITUTET, UPPSALA 2013

INDEXING TERMS:
Higher education
Aid programmes
Capacity building
Research and development
Career development
Labour mobility
Gender equality
Mozambique

ISSN 0280-2171
ISBN 978-91-7106-743-2
Language editing: Peter Colenbrander
© The author, The Nordic Africa Institute
Production: Byrå4
Print on demand, Lightning Source UK Ltd.

Contents

Tables

Polars

Diagrams

In the competitive global knowledge economy, highly qualified individuals are increasingly recognised as being the key to development. In particular, doctorate holders are not only the most qualified in terms of educational attainment, but also those specifically trained to be at the forefront of innovation and in a position to drive advances in science, technology and knowledge of society. In developing countries with relatively weak research structures, not least with regard to PhD graduates, the training of PhDs has been intimately linked to the reproduction of human capacity in national research systems.

National expenditure on research remains low in many African countries. According to UNESCO data, the GERD/GDP ratio in most sub-Saharan countries ranges between 0.1 and 0.4 per cent (UNESCO 2010:280). The pool of researchers varies significantly between countries in absolute and relative terms. Compared to developed countries, the proportion of researchers per million inhabitants is exceptionally low. South Africa excluded, one finds an average of 57.5 researchers per million in sub-Saharan countries, compared to an average of 3,656 researchers per million in developed countries (UNESCO 2010:8).

Faced with this daunting data on the supply of researchers in sub-Saharan countries, there is no doubt that highly skilled individuals are a very important and sensitive strategic national resource. The absence of data on the mobility and career development of these individuals in most African countries is hence quite remarkable.

This study examines the mobility of PhD graduates funded under the Swedish development aid program to build institutional research capacity in Mozambique from 1990 to 2013. Principal areas of investigation are extent and direction of geographic, sectoral and vertical mobility, perception and individual rationales for mobility and career choices and experience of the so-called "sandwich model".

The study builds on a data set consisting of 159 traced individuals. A web-based questionnaire has formed the basis for the quantitative analysis. From this sample a number of respondents have been strategically selected for deep interviews. The survey and interviews have been analysed using a multi-methods approach. The study situates academic career development and mobility within the changing role and function of research and higher education in society. Particular attention has been given to gender relations, scientific discipline and country of training.

Main results indicate a remarkably low mobility among the PhD graduates, geographical as well as sectoral. Regardless of gender and academic discipline, a significant share of researchers trained in the program during the period 1990-2012 has remained at Eduardo Mondlane University (UEM). Even though the attainment of a PhD has meant a lot to many of the graduates, the degree seems to have been more important in boosting status and self-confidence than for the actual work. The relatively low number of staff members holding PhD degrees at UEM has meant fast career development for some of the graduates, both in their departments and in the university administration. Notably, women represent a significantly lower share of those who have achieved high position at UEM. The willingness to conduct research is much greater than the resources and time available. The great majority of graduates have continued to do research, but on a quite small scale. Salary, working conditions and degree of independence stand out as the principal sources of dissatisfaction among the graduates. Supplementary income from consultancies seems to be widespread among graduates and is an accepted part of academic life at UEM.

Insufficient local resources for research and co-supervision at UEM seem to be the most problematic areas in the training situation, regardless of gender, discipline or country of training (Sweden and South Africa). A positive attitude to the idea and premises of the sandwich model, but findings also indicate that the mobile character of the modality has different effects on women and men. There was a significantly higher level of dissatisfaction among graduates and candidates that have done or were doing their training at South African universities, compared to their Swedish equivalents. The main discriminatory expressions at work at UEM seem be on the basis of family situation and position at the workplace. Women seem to experience discrimination in these areas significantly more than men.

Abbreviations of acronyms

AAU	Association of African Universities
AU	African Union
CDH	Careers for Doctorate Holders
COMESA	Common Market for Eastern and Southern African Countries
EAC	East African Community
ECOWAS	Economic Community of West African States
ERA	European Research Area
EU	European Union
FDI	Foreign Direct Investment
GATS	General Agreement on Trade in Services
GDP	Gross Domestic Product
GERD	Gross Domestic Expenditure on Science and Technology
HRST	Human Resources in Science and Technology
IICT	Scientific and Technological Research Institute
ICT	Information and Communications Technology
ISRI	Higher Institute for International Relations
IMF	International Monetary Fund
ISCO	International Standard Classification of Occupations
MHEST	Ministry for Higher Education, Science and Technology
MORE	Mobility and Career Paths for Doctorate Holders in Europe
MOSTIS	Mozambican Science, Technology and Innovation Strategy
NEPAD	New Partnership for Africa's Development
ODA	Official Development Assistance
OECD	Organization for Economic Cooperation and Development
PEES	Strategic Plan for Higher Education
PRSP	Poverty Reduction Strategy Paper
R&D	Research and Development
RBM	Results-Based Management
SADC	Southern African Development Community
SAREC	Swedish Agency for Research Cooperation
Sida	Swedish International Development Agency
STEM	Science, Technology, Engineering and Mathematics
UEM	Eduardo Mondlane University
UNESCO	United Nations Educational, Scientific and Cultural Organization
UN	United Nations
UP	Pedagogic University
WEI	World Education Indicators
WTO	World Trade Organization

In the competitive global knowledge economy, highly qualified individuals are increasingly recognised as being the key to development. In particular, doctorate holders are not only the most qualified in terms of educational attainment, but also those specifically trained to be at the forefront of innovation and in a position to drive advances in science, technology and knowledge of society. In developing countries with relatively weak research structures, not least with regard to PhD graduates, the training of PhDs has been intimately linked to the reproduction of human capacity in national research systems. However, a number of factors affecting mobility and alternative career paths for PhD graduates have increasingly challenged the connection between PhD training and research capacity at universities in many such countries. Of the many factors reported in recent literature, the following stand out: i) inadequate resources for research at many national universities, always a problem but now gradually worsened by the current trend towards massification in higher education; ii) the increased policy-driven internationalisation of research and higher education, leading to increased competition and mobility within the international research community; iii) an escalating number of market-driven private higher education institutions in many developing countries, offering no or limited research resources; and iv) increased demand from other sectors in society, private and public, for trained researchers to meet the requirements of the global knowledge economy, for example, the innovation capacity of enterprises.

A number of international donors have a long record of supporting research capacity-building in African institutions, some with PhD training as a central component. There are, however, significant differences between donors in terms of scope, design and ownership of these programs, arising from different views of how institutional capacity building should be achieved. The principal rationale behind Swedish support has been that each country should have at least one university capable of expanding national research and the higher education sphere. Accordingly, the training of PhDs (using a sandwich program intended to sustain the links with the home institution) constitutes a core component in fostering the capacity to formulate and conduct research of relevance and quality. This approach aims at tackling capacity building more holistically by going beyond the individual researcher and also by decentralising most responsibilities, administrative and substantive, to partners in the collaborating country.

Sida has been engaged in supporting PhD training in low-income African countries for over three decades, in the process generating a considerable number of PhD graduates. Despite the duration of this PhD training as a core activity in these programs, knowledge of the long-term outcomes of this strategic investment is quite limited. This is particularly true of the mobility and career development of this group of graduates, a significant indicator of the outcome of this type of aid. Consequently, comparative analysis of the outcomes of different approaches to building research capacity has not been feasible. No Swedish or partner institutions have established mechanisms for keeping track of returning graduates. On the whole, studies looking at modes of mobility and career choices among PhDs, particularly in the developing world, are rare. Longitudinal studies on the qualitative aspects of mobility and career choices in developing countries are almost non-existent.

1. African countries in transition: Knowledge-driven society and role of highly skilled individuals

Today, the main determinant of poverty in Africa is neither lack of natural resources nor geographical marginality, but the lack of skilled individuals to produce added value, make use of existing technology and develop context-specific innovations and solutions.

According to the IMF's latest review of the world economy (World Economic Outlook), Africa continues to consolidate its position as host of the most rapidly advancing economies in the world (IMF 2013). In the last decade, six of the top ten fastest growing economies were to be found on the continent. Economic and political conditions in many countries are becoming more conducive to economic growth and change, as indicated by increased FDI, better conditions for private capital investment, greater institutional diversity, accelerating regional economic integration[1] and growing trade with Asian countries in particular.[2] These developments have led to more stable macro-political environments as compared to the 1980s and 1990s. Democratisation and political liberalisation are slowly making progress in most African countries.

Africa's current macroeconomic performance is indeed impressive, but tends to obscure the development deficiencies remaining in many African societies, which affect large segments of the population.[3] Despite impressive growth rates (up to 6 per cent per annum in some countries), real GDP growth seems not to have translated into equal benefits for the population. The distribution figure for economic growth has its equivalent in the figures for income distribution: six of the ten countries scoring highest on the inequality index are in Africa. A recent Gini index measuring income inequality in Africa yields a high total of 45 (on a scale of 0 to 100), which is only marginally better compared to the situation 30 years ago (Anyanwu 2012). Not surprisingly, the non-beneficiaries are to be found among the low-income sectors of the population, predominantly in rural areas. In Mozambique, the mean share of the lowest 20 per cent of the population is 5.2 per cent of total national income, while the upper 20 per cent accounts for 51.5 per cent (Africa Development Bank Group 2012). Consequently, economic growth has so far had relatively meagre results in terms of poverty reduction. The World Bank's "PovCalNet" database indicates a doubling of the

---

1. COMESA, EAC, ECOWAS and SADC.
2. In 2009, China surpassed the US as Africa's largest trading partner. However, both countries still lag the EU in terms of trade volumes. It is expected that China will become Africa's leading trading partner over the next five years (OECD 2012).
3. Interestingly, a recurrent theme in many World Bank analyses and recommendations is the stress on growth and equality as objectives in tension: countries must choose between them, since each is seen as an obstacle to the other (Samoff *et al.* 2004:36).

absolute number of impoverished people since 1981 (Thorbecke 2013).[4] African countries account for 34 of the 50 nations on the UN's list of least developed countries. Mozambique can be found near the very bottom of the list, placed 185 out of 187 (Human Development Index 2013).

Without going into detail about the multidimensional developmental opportunities and deficiencies in African countries, it is evident that current development is more than ever coupled with the overall challenge of building sufficient and relevant capacity for global participation and competition and, on the other hand, finding appropriate political tools to overcome growing economic and social inequalities within society. More particularly, there is a need for institutional capacity for competitive and strategic exchanges with foreign investors and trade partners, whose financial inflows represent a significant part of current overall economic growth. Due to intensifying global competition for natural resources, many African countries now face favourable conditions for development and catch-up, but lack the institutional capacity for strategic coordination and long-term social planning. This insufficiency is intimately linked to the challenge of overcoming the increasing inequalities in incomes and wealth, which, if not dealt with, will arrest development and give rise to social destabilisation and political unrest.

An indispensable factor in tackling these challenges is knowledge. This was formerly treated as a subordinate factor in development economics, "as something 'exogenous' and readily available on 'shelves' as a public good (Mkandawire 2011). Now, knowledge and knowledge production, as manifested in areas such as R&D, entrepreneurship and innovation capacity, have become a top policy priority for any government. The premises of the knowledge-led economy have been increasingly applied by the EU as a tool for growth and job creation. In the Europe 2020 strategy, the European Commission aims to turn the EU "into a smart, sustainable and inclusive economy that delivers high levels of employment, productivity and social cohesion" (EU 2010). Seven so-called "flagship initiatives" accompany the strategy. Supporting the "Smart Growth" flagship is the "Innovation Union," which provides a framework for research and innovation for the development of products and services that create growth and jobs (EU Commission 2012). The ERA has been assigned a key role in realising the Innovative Union. Of interest to this study is the fact that the ERA situates the individual at the core of innovation activity. As the EU Commission policy document notes:

> ERA should inspire the best talents to enter research careers in Europe [and] enable European researchers to develop strong links with partners around the world, so that Europe benefits from the progress of knowledge worldwide, con-

---

4. Since the late 1980s, the number of people living on less than US$ 1 per day in sub-Saharan Africa rose by 70 million, reaching 290 million in 1998, over 46 per cent of the total population (African Development Bank 2012).

tributes to global development and takes a leading role in international initiatives to solve global issues … increase[d] mobility of knowledge workers, supporting training and ensuring attractive careers are central goals of ERA. (EU Commission 2012)

Highly qualified individuals are thus recognised as key in the knowledge-economy. Of these, doctorate holders are not only the most qualified in terms of educational attainment, but are also those specifically trained to be at the forefront of innovation by driving advances in science, technology and knowledge of society. Consequently, the strategic and often demanding investments made in these individuals have increased policy interest in their mobility and career development. Adding to this growing interest is the intensifying international competition for highly skilled people, such as doctorate holders, not only among academic research institutions but also from other prospective employers looking for specific skills in their workforce. Strategies and programs aimed to attract and retain these individuals have hence become essential to sustaining competitive advantages in the knowledge economy. For instance, in the EU these considerations have been given effect in the creation of a European partnership aiming to improve the mobility of researchers and the flow of knowledge, improve career prospects for researchers in Europe, and, not least, to retain researchers in Europe and attract talented non-European researchers (EU Commission 2008).

For such programs to be effective, they must build studies of the mobility and career development of doctorate holders and their contribution to scientific and economic development. Although there is a considerable literature on the current changes within the global research and higher education sector (many with a potential impact on the mobility and career development of PhD graduates), and despite the growing attention by many governments on the link between society and academia, studies on the scale, direction, driving forces and rationale behind mobility and career choices of PhD graduates are comparably few in number and limited in scope (Hoffman 2008). Access to research based knowledge is still both limited and uneven, largely because of the lack of internationally comparable data and the fact that standard statistical sources are too meagre to produce robust results for this particular group of individuals (Jerven 2013, OECD 2007).[5]

---

5. "Researcher" is not identified as a distinct category in ISCO. An additional complication is the fact that there are two accepted international definitions of "researcher": the OECD (Canberra Manual 1995) definition based on the concept of HRST and the OECD Frascati Manual (2002), in terms of which OECD member-state R&D statistics are collected.

2. Objectives of the study

This study responds to the need for increased knowledge on mobility and career development among PhD graduates funded under the Swedish program in order to enhance Swedish policy on development cooperation and in areas related to the interplay between academia and society in developing countries. It aims to map and analyse longitudinally and comparatively the modes of, and rationales for, mobility and career development among PhD graduates to build institutional research capacity in Mozambique from 1990 to date.

The study has three principal areas of investigation: i) extent and direction of mobility (geographic, sectoral and vertical) over time, ii) perceptions and individual rationales for mobility and career choices and iii) experience of the sandwich model.

In the first area of investigation the following principal research questions will be examined: In which areas and in what positions are Sida-funded PhD graduates at present? What do individual circumstances look like in terms of geographical mobility and mobility between sectors from the date of graduation up to the present? Can specific patterns of mobility be identified in terms of gender, age and date of graduation? From a longitudinal perspective, are there differences in mobility among PhD graduates from different time periods and across disciplines?

In the second area of investigation the following principal research questions will be explored: How do individual PhD graduates reflect on alternatives for mobility and career path linked with their academic position/rank? How do they relate these alternatives to conditions in academia and society at large (gender, age, socio-economic background, nationality and date of graduation)? What are the driving forces behind individual mobility and career choices and to what extent can these be linked to the systematic changes in higher education and research and different donor approaches to support PhD training?

In the third area of investigation the following principal research questions will be explored: How have PhD graduates experienced the sandwich model[6]? Experiences from the time spent in Sweden and at the home institution. Can specific experiential patterns be identified in terms of gender, age, date of graduation, position at home institution and across disciplines?

---

6. The Sandwich model is a support modality allowing for mobility (e.g. six months stays in each country) between the institution in the country of training and the institution in the country of origin during the entire period of training. The model has since long been applied by Sida as the main modality when supporting PhD-training.

3. Methodology

This study covers PhD graduates and candidates in Sida's bilateral program to support research capacity-building in Mozambique during the period 1990-2012. The year 1990 was chosen as a starting point since it marks the beginning of the major changes associated with commodification, privatisation and massification in the African higher education and research systems (GUNI 2008). Hypothetically, these alterations have over time and in different ways and degrees impacted the mobility and career choices of PhD holders.

The total data set consists of 159 individuals mainly traced through existing lists of UEM graduates; lists, registers and supervisors at relevant institutions and departments in Sweden and South Africa; and social and professional networks of graduates in different disciplines. The main challenge has not been in the identification of the individual per se but in contacting him/her through a current e-mail address, required for forwarding the web-based questionnaire (see appendix). E-mail addresses not in use have been a recurrent problem. From the initial sample, PhD graduates were strategically selected for deep interviews, which took place over three weeks in March 2013. The number of interviews was determined in relation to the response rate for the web-based questionnaire and to achieve broad representativeness in terms of gender, age, scientific discipline, year of graduation and country of graduation/training. For a more detailed description of the methodology (sample, method and limitations) see appendix.

4. Theoretical framework and previous research

4.1 Academic careers and mobility in the global knowledge economy

Academic mobility and career development is not constructed in a social, historical or geopolitical vacuum. Instead, it is produced and negotiated within various intersecting and shifting power relations, both local and global. Of particular interest for this study is the way in which increasing global demands for competition and accountability play out in local contexts and academic cultures with differing conditions for mobility and research. However, little is known about how international donor activities intersect, in perhaps opposing and contradictory ways, with the global policy demands of the knowledge economy and, ultimately, how these circumstances are experienced and perceived by the academic. Against this backdrop, how can we understand the career paths and rationales of academics from the Global South?

Overall, the study situates academic mobility within the changing role and function of research and higher education in society and the greater steering of research priorities, the "commercialisation of research" and the increased emphasis on accountability and audit – in short, the shift from the "traditional" to the "relevant" academy (Benner and Sorlin 2008, Kogan and Teichler 2007, Nowotny *et al.* 2006). Further, the study will also take into account existing research on massification, commodification and privatisation in African higher education and research systems, all of which point to the challenge of maintaining quality in education and research (Jaishree 2004, Saunders 2007, Stromquist 2000).

4.2 Previous research on mobility of researchers

The majority of existing studies focus on patterns of mobility and career development among researchers in the Global North, mainly the US and Europe. Major studies of European researcher mobility are the Study on the mobility patterns and career paths of EU researchers (MORE)[7] and Careers for Doctorate Holders (CDH)[8]. Both studies use survey-based sources trying to answer questions about mobility in relation to brain drain, brain gain and brain circulation. The main focus is the correspondence between number of PhD graduates and labour market needs, attractiveness of national labour markets, how well the skills of highly educated people are used by society and, not least, how attractive alternative career paths are to this category of individuals.

---

7. MORE is funded by the European Commission (DG Research) and is carried out by an international consortium led by IDEA Consult. The study builds on existing data (IISER project) but also collects and analyses new data on the stock and flow of European researchers.

8. CDH is an OECD collaborative project with the UNESCO Institute for Statistics and Eurostat aimed at developing internationally comparable indicators on the careers and mobility of doctorate holders (OECD 2007)

The main results from the MORE study are that 56 per cent of the sampled PhD graduates working in higher education and research had spent at least three consecutive months in another country. Two-thirds of these researchers were men[9]. Of the incentives for mobility, professionally related motives such as personal research agendas, opportunities for career advancement and salary exerted the greatest influence. Issues such as language, administrative barriers, social security systems and childcare were generally found to be of subordinate importance in the decision to become geographically mobile. (MORE 2010). In large part, the findings of the OECD study were similar to the MORE study, in that they display relatively high mobility among European citizens with PhDs. As previously mentioned, it is worth noting that men represent two thirds of the mobility in the MORE study.[10]

Another relevant study is the GlobSci survey looking at 16 so-called "core" countries (all in the Global North), which surveyed corresponding authors of scientific articles written during a given year in four science fields. The study, which focuses on inflow and outflow patterns in relation to scientific production and collaboration, indicates that up 40 per cent of researchers in some of the surveyed countries were immigrants.[11] A similar figure is given for the maintenance of research links to the country of origin among foreign-born researchers, indicating the spillover effects of mobility (Franzoni *et al.* 2012).

Besides these large surveys, one finds several smaller studies covering mobility to and from specific countries, or the mobility of defined categories of researchers. Some studies have tried to grasp the complex relationship between mobility, network building and scientific production (Melin 2004, Jonkers and Tijssen 2008), while others have looked specifically at the mobility of highly

9. Close to 30 per cent had a recent (at least once during the past three years) experience of mobility. Age, years since graduation and family situation were shown to be affecting variables: the younger the person, the greater the mobility. Individuals who had stayed abroad as students were more frequently mobile as researchers. Concerning sectoral mobility, 17 per cent had moved between public and private sectors, with science and technology graduates being over-represented in this category.

10. Over a period of ten years, 15–30 per cent of them had worked abroad, mainly in other European countries. As with the MORE study, it was found that researchers in science and technology were more likely to engage in research than their counterparts in the social sciences and humanities, who had greater mobility towards non-research sectors in society (Auriol 2010).

11. This figure is supported by a previous study of postdoctoral researchers working in Europe in the life sciences, which showed that 43 per cent of researchers were working in a country other than their country of origin (Empirica 2005). These figures correspond fairly well with figures for the US indicating that 41.6 per cent of doctorate holders working in science and engineering in 2009 were born abroad (National Science Board 2012 in Stephan 2012). Approximately 48 per cent of all PhDs awarded in the US went to non-citizens and almost 60 per cent of all postdoctoral students working in the US are non-citizens (Stephan 2012). The movement of EU doctorates to the US is relatively high, while the reverse flow is negligible (IISER 2007).

productive researchers (Hunter *et al.* 2009, Levin and Stephan 1999, Laudel 2005).[12]

Research on gender and academic mobility reveals that there are gender differences in the direction and scope of academic mobility and that possibilities and hindrances for transnational academic mobility are gendered. Factors related to partnership, children, dual careers constellations, as well as to social class and academic integration construct differing conditions for women and men academics. Taken together these processes are resulting in inequalities in the accumulation of international cultural and social capital (Leemann 2010). In this vein, research from a German context reveals that participation of researchers in transnational academic mobility, their experiences and perceived outcomes vary by gender. In this context the academic world of female researchers tends to be less international than that of their male colleagues. Significant variations over time regarding length of staying, source of country, subject and career stage are main results indicating the need for further research (Jöns 2010).

The representativeness and reliability of existing studies on the mobility of PhD graduates are debatable. Both their geographical and disciplinary coverage is too limited to allow for general assumptions about movement patterns and, particularly, driving forces for this specific group. It is evident that the recent increased policy focus by governments in the Global North on highly skilled people as drivers for economic growth has spurred research efforts to statistically map inflows and outflows. Apart from deliberate limitations in geographical coverage, most studies offer quite limited disciplinary coverage, in accordance with current policy stress on the STEM sciences as keys to economic growth. Survey-based studies of mobility patterns for PhD graduates in medicine, social science and the humanities are still scant. Existing studies also face validity problems. Despite large population samples, they suffer from exceptionally low response rates.[13]

The inconsistency of statistical databases across countries has also affected comparative studies, for example regarding the definition and classification of central variables such the socioeconomic indexing of researchers, and whether they are foreign-born or in their country of origin. Because of difficulties in tracking individuals working abroad, most countries lack information on the mobility patterns of PhD graduates born in their countries. Existing studies tend to focus primarily on PhD graduates still working in academia or in other sites of scientific production. Cross-country comparative studies of sectoral mo-

---

12. Highly productive researchers seem to be more mobile: 50 per cent of the world's often-cited physics PhDs work in a country in which they were not born (Hunter *et al.* 2009). Levin and Stephan (1999) found that this group of scientists working in the US was more likely to be foreign born and educated than the underlying population of US scientists.

13. Reportedly, the MORE project response rate was only 11 per cent (Franzoni *et al.* 2012).

bility, for instance those PhD graduates that have left academic life for positions in other sectors, seem to have attracted less scholarly attention. One of the more serious criticisms of existing mobility studies is their strong preference for quantitatively based surveys as the sole method of data collection. While this may be suitable for mapping mobility as physical movement from one place to another, it has limitations in capturing and explaining incentives for and driving forces behind mobility, which may be of equal interest from a policy perspective. Consequently, many studies fail to provide a nuanced and balanced picture of the non-quantitative variables involved in mobility. In general, there are few studies examining international and sectoral mobility in relation to other aspects of individual career development.

Africa is very modestly represented in the research literature on academic mobility and career development. The few studies that do exist mainly discuss mobility in relation to the problem of brain drain, and often are based on quite unreliable estimates of graduate outflows Mainly because of the lack of reliable and relevant data for comparative statistical processing, it is hard to find systematic mapping studies of the mobility of postgraduates and PhD graduates in particular. Longitudinal studies on qualitative aspects of mobility and career development focused on low-income countries are almost non-existent (Tremblay 2009).

Given the increasing strategic value of highly skilled individuals such as PhD graduates and their limited number in Africa, the absence of studies of how these individuals orient themselves in terms of career choices is remarkable. It is also remarkable that the extensive and long-term support of international donors for PhD training as the basis for building research capacity has not given rise to studies, despite the increased focus on Result-Based Management (RBM) in international donor policy. Policy-makers are thus left to speculate on the driving forces for career development and mobility among this strategic group of individuals, as well as their contribution to the development of society.

4.3 Previous research on gender in higher education and research

In her research on gender equity in Commonwealth higher education, Louise Morley (2005, 2006) notes that there are three bodies of literature that seldom relate to one another. First, the literature on gender, development and education rarely touch on higher education. Second, the literature on higher education in "developing countries" tends to be organised in gender-neutral terms.

The third body of literature focuses on gender in higher education. Mostly developed in the Global North, this research has focused on several interrelated themes ranging from social psychological approaches to studies of gendered constructions of academic identities and large studies on gender differences in academic careers (Thomas 1999, Husu 2001 Zuckermann 1991, Thutkoushian

1999, NSF report 2003). The results indicate that women's career paths are more winding than men's career paths and include pauses due to childcare as well as movements in and out from academia. Women report more experiences on discrimination based on gender and existing research indicates that women are exposed to more discrimination based on gender (Zuckermann 1991, Wold and Vennerås 1996, Thutkoushian 1999, NSF report 2003).

The ways in which gender interacts with other social relations in the production and reproduction of inequalities in higher education is an under-researched area. The existing literature, particularly that which references Black feminism and critical race studies, has mainly emerged in the Anglo-Saxon world. In this context, intersections of gender, race and class, and how these mutually impact on the possibilities and hindrances for black and coloured women's careers has been at the centre of analysis (see, for example, Mirza 1989, Muhns *et al.* 2012).

In an African context, intersectional research on gender in higher education is not a mainstream approach. Many African feminists have highlighted the importance of focusing on gender in research on inequalities, since this has historically often been under-represented relative to racialised inequalities (Bennet 2002, Mabukela & Magubane 2004). In the Nordic context, the situation is rather the reverse, with gender being privileged relative to racialised/ethicised inequalities in research on inequalities in Higher education (Mählck 2012). In addition, Universities in Sweden and Mozambique are facing different challenges in relation to the global knowledge economy, situated as they are in different higher education and research landscapes. As such gender relations in academic careers and mobility patterns are played out in very different geopolitical, social and university contexts. Against this backdrop this study has been inspired by an intersectional sensitive approach to analysing power relations in academic careers. (see also Yuval Davis 2006 for a similar approach).

4.4 A theory of limited difference in academic careers
The theory of limited differences offers an established way of understanding differences in academic careers (Cole and Singer 1991). At its core is the perception of an academic career as a social construct needing to be studied in longitudinal perspective. Another central feature is that the theory suggests an academic career is shaped and negotiated in conjunction with everyday academic work life. From this perspective, careers are shaped by small, even seemingly trivial, events in everyday academic work rather than from significant emotional, institutional or embodied crises or unexpected incidents, although these may also significantly influence career paths and mobility. Furthermore, it is the cumulative effect of these small events and the reactions to them that create differing career paths and mobility.

The theory of limited difference provides a framework for studying academic career paths longitudinally while also being sensitive to local context. However, it is not designed to investigate hierarchical relations or the ways in which power is produced and negotiated in everyday work lives. In her research on gender relations in the Commonwealth University context, Morley (2005) suggests a different framework, inspired by the French philosopher Michel Foucault's notion of micro-politics. In her reading of Foucault, micro-politics "can help to reveal the increasingly subtle and sophisticated ways in which dominance is achieved in academic organisations" (Morley 1999 in Morley 2006:544).

Our report suggests a synthesis of these perspectives as a way forward. Micro-politics can serve as an analytical entry point for researching power and privilege within a broader investigation of researchers' careers as longitudinal events, shaped and reshaped by a series of cumulative events and reactions. This conception of academic careers enables sensitive analysis of how local power relations are produced in everyday work as well as how these relations are connected to larger structures of inequality in society at large and also how these processes interact and shape academic careers.

5. Situating PhD graduates in the Mozambican research and higher education system

5.1 Research and higher education in the African development

An accurate understanding of the patterns of and incentives for mobility and career development for PhD graduates can be achieved only if the analysis is contextually placed within the overall economic, political and social development of the society. Since these individuals are specifically trained to conduct research, it is crucial to position their mobility and career choices in relation to current and past developments in the research and higher education system, both at national and international level.

Historically, from being important institutional symbols (not least physically) of nation building in the early years of independence[14], African universities gradually lost ground in the 1970s and 1980s. A number of explanations have been given for this reversion. Makandawire argues that two factors were of particular importance: the difficulty in marrying one-party rule and academic freedom and the lack of consensus on what constituted relevant research. "African governments tended to view universities as intended for the production of 'manpower' necessary to indigenise the civil service … [I]f they thought about research at all they wanted research that was relevant to 'development and nation building'" (Makandawire 2011:15). This diminishing role of higher education and research in development culminated with the World Bank's *coup de grace* in the late 1980s, when it declared that the social returns from higher education were low in comparison to basic education (World Bank 1988:14–23). The policy priority of primary education was institutionalised during 1990 international conference on education for all (Samoff and Carrol 2004:5). This conclusion was soon taken up by international donors, which changed their policies and conditionalities for supporting higher education. Consequently, higher education was absent from most countries' poverty reduction strategy papers (PRSP), Mozambique being an exception (Bloom *et al.* 2005). Coupled with political turmoil and economic regression in the 1970s and 1980s, these factors contributed significantly to the decay of higher education institutions in Africa. Reportedly, public recurrent expenditure per tertiary student fell from $6,461 in 1975 to $2,365 in 1983 (World Bank 1988:143). For obvious reasons, this diminished recognition and decline affected the situation of staff members at universities, as well as the training of postgraduates, not least PhDs. Though empirically based studies of rates and directions of mobility are lacking, there

---

14. The 1962 Tananariva Conference on the theme of development of higher education in Africa agreed on the universities' key role in national development. A workshop in Accra ten years later on creating the African university identified two main purposes for the university: 1) establishing identity and links with the past; 2) addressing the practical need for high level manpower and the production of knowledge and skills to create wealth and modernise African societies (Beintema *et al.* 1998).

is a common understanding among scholars that this situation contributed to significant outflows of staff from universities to other countries or other forms of employment (World Bank 2004:6).

Greatly influenced by the changing World Bank stance, the policy pendulum has in the last decade swung back in favour of research and higher education, especially the latter. Responding to criticisms of a too narrow and partly counter-productive focus on basic education, the bank has gradually begun to advocate a more holistic approach to higher education (World Bank 2002). One obvious defect in the one-sided emphasis on basic education was the problem of inter-connectedness of the education system, a problem that particularly concerned the role of higher education institutions as providers of qualified teachers. Of primary relevance to this study is not the growing recognition of the intercon-nectedness within the education system, but the way in which higher education and research have come to be viewed as preconditions for development and positioning in a knowledge-driven society. This perception mirrors the current policy positions of most OECD countries and other emerging economies. Several recent empirical studies note a distinct correlation between enrolment rates in higher education and growth in national income (Urama 2009).[15] Important to understanding the positioning of highly skilled individuals such as PhD gradu-ates is the bank's statement on the main factors for achieving knowledge-driven development: a country's macroeconomic incentives and institutional regime, its ICT infrastructure, its national innovation system and the quality of its skilled workforce (World Bank 2002:23–41). In fact, the supply of skilled individuals is perhaps the most important factor. The position of PhD graduates, who are both the product and agents of the knowledge society, is naturally central, not least as a key resource for innovation and innovation systems. While research is not explicitly addressed in the bank's revised policy directives, it is recognised as an indispensable component of the innovation system.

The correlation between access to advanced knowledge and global economic positioning has increasingly influenced policy development in many African countries. There is growing awareness among governments that to sustain cur-rent levels of economic growth knowledge needs to be developed, transmitted and deployed in more efficient ways. Where new technology is introduced, the demand for skilled individuals will rise. Consequently, research and higher edu-cation institutions in many African countries have over the past ten to fifteen years witnessed a new dawn and a revitalised role in development.

Since the mid-1990s, there has been a dramatic increase in the number of students in higher education in Africa, an expansion that has in many respects changed the role of the university in society. From being a quite exclusive in-

---

15. On the downside, some studies show that the relative cost of higher education per student as a proportion of national GDP is higher in Africa than in developed countries (Moyer 2009).

stitution for the reproduction of a distinct social elite, higher education has been transformed into something comparable to a global service, with an annual turnover of millions of students (Altbach 2008).[16] In sub-Saharan Africa, the number of students has almost tripled in the last 20 years.[17] Increased demand has initially been met through existing limited capacity, which in many cases has resulted in the unfounded exclusion of highly qualified students. This problem persists, notwithstanding a dramatic increase in the number and types of higher learning institution in many African countries, including Mozambique. Institutional differentiation has meant both new directions (horizontal differentiation) and specialisation (vertical differentiation).

A significant feature of current African higher education is the dramatic increase in market-driven private institutions. In Africa, private institutions are still less prevalent than in, for example, Latin America and Asia, but the growth rate is higher. In countries such as Botswana, Namibia, Rwanda, Burundi and Angola, private institutions account for more than 40 per cent of the total number of registered students. In Tanzania, Uganda and Ethiopia, private options are much fewer (Varghese 2004:10–14). In one respect, growing privatisation and marketisation in higher education are an indication of the inability of the public systems to meet increased demand from individual students and society, both quantatively and qualitatively. The emergence of private options can also be understood in terms of autonomy. Private institutions are less sensitive to political and economic governance issues and the instability that can undermine supply and quality. One consequence of increasing privatisation and marketisation in higher education is that they also affect public institutions, which are gradually forced to abandon their traditional non-profit role in favour of income-generating commercial activities (Mamdani 2007). The growing number of private institutions has also occasioned wage competition with public institutions for qualified staff members, not least PhD graduates.

Internationalisation has become a buzzword in policy circles on higher education and research. Even though international relations and exchange have long been an essential aspect of university activities, academic, political and cultural incentives have gradually been superseded by economic incentives. Governments increasingly view student and research mobility as a key component of

---

16. The rapid growth in higher education can be mainly attributed to increased access, participation and success at primary and secondary levels, demographic trends and the increased demand for specialised knowledge. According to UNESCO's World Education Indicators (WEI), participation in secondary education increased on average by 39 per cent between 1995 and 2003. High birth rate is also an important factor. In many African countries more than half the population is under 30 (UNESCO 2006).

17. Despite significant increases, sub-Saharan Africa remains the region with the lowest number of registered students in higher education.

economic growth. Cross-border education has become a marketable commodity, indeed part of trade negotiations under GATS (GUNI 2008:121).

Understanding the incentives for PhD mobility and career paths requires some comment on the challenges flowing from the recent expansion of higher education institutions in Africa. Generally, it is clear most countries lack the capacity to meet the increased demand. Particularly worrisome is the shortage of qualified postgraduate teachers. This shortfall is mainly due to lack of capacity in postgraduate education and the inability to attract and retain qualified personnel due to low wages and poor working conditions. Ineffective management and administration means that many universities fail to increase the accessibility, quality and relevance of the training offered. Furthermore, faculty and department managers are rarely administratively trained and lack knowledge of strategic planning, research management, financial planning, human resource management and performance management. Waves of retirement are also a contributing factor.

Years of political deprioritisation and economic austerity have undermined the quality of training and research at many universities. Faced with increasing political demands for mass production, universities now stand ill-equipped, with inadequate facilities and infrastructure; limited and outdated library resources, technological equipment and instructional materials; outdated curricula; and, not least, insufficient and unqualified teachers. Inadequate resources have also meant that many African universities lack access to globally produced knowledge, making them internationally isolated and with less potential to catch up. There are also concerns about curriculum relevance and lack of coherence between university and society, caused by an imbalance between supply and demand in certain subject areas. Despite the mass intake of undergraduate students, the numbers of Master's and Doctoral students remains relatively small.[18]

Equality and discrimination are other areas receiving little attention. Although the number of women in higher education, both as students and teachers, has increased in recent years, the proportion has not. The low proportion of women is particularly noteworthy in science and technology.

Of particular importance to PhD graduates is that policy prioritisation of training has weakened research and innovation capacity at many higher education institutions. Researchers have fewer resources and less time to engage in research. What is particularly worrying is that this affects already weak structures. Even though many sub-Saharan countries have begun to recognise the importance of investment in Science and Technology (S&T) the high priority afforded train-

---

18. One problem is the low enrolment rates in science, engineering and technology. The figures vary between countries, but indicate that on average less than 30 per cent of students enrol in these faculties. In Uganda and Tanzania, the figure is 16 per cent. On the other hand, high enrolments in the social sciences and humanities have resulted in a large surplus of these graduates on the job market, leading to high unemployment (Teferre and Altbach. 2004).

ing has depleted already insufficient public allocations for research. Consequently, dependence on external financial support, which often targets short-term goals, remains high, as does exclusion from global scientific production.

With few exceptions, national expenditure on research remains low. Only South Africa is close to reaching the 1 per cent GERD/GDP ratio recommended by UNESCO and the AU. According to UNESCO data, the GERD/GDP ratio in most sub-Saharan countries ranges between 0.1 and 0.4 per cent (UNESCO 2010:280).[19] The pool of researchers varies significantly between countries in absolute and relative terms.[20] Compared to developed countries, the proportion of researchers per million inhabitants is exceptionally low. South Africa excluded, one finds an average of 57.5 researchers per million in sub-Saharan countries, compared to an average of 3,656 researchers per million in developed countries (UNESCO 2010:8).[21] In sum, faced with this daunting data on the supply of researchers in sub-Saharan countries, there is no doubt that highly skilled individuals are a very important and sensitive strategic national resource. The absence of data on the mobility and career development of these individuals in most African countries is hence quite remarkable.

The limited number of researchers has a direct effect on scientific production. Sub-Saharan countries' share of global scientific output is somewhat over 1 per cent.[22] There are several plausible explanations of why this production has not increased. The best explanation is the policy focus over the last decade on undergraduate training, at the expense of research. Training and research now compete for resources not only financial but also human, at universities. The staff trained specifically to conduct research, the PhD graduates, are required to allocate most of their working time to teaching. If little time is spent in devising and conducting research, funding (both public and external) will decline and few scientific publications will follow.[23]

19. Measuring the GERD/GDP ratio has also proven difficult because of lack of data. Many countries have no record of the share of GDP to R&D (UNESCO 2010:281).
20. Nigeria and South Africa host the largest absolute number of researchers, but proportionately Botswana, Senegal and Guinea are above or at the same level. What is striking is the significant proportionate variation between countries, ranging from 8 researchers per million inhabitants in Niger to 942 per million inhabitants in Botswana (UNESCO 2010:284).
21. The proportion of female researchers, particularly in STEM sciences, remains low in most countries. With the exception of Cape Verde (52.3 per cent) and Lesotho (55.7 per cent), the average proportion of female researchers is around 25 per cent.
22. This figure obscures significant variations between countries. South Africa accounts for almost half of scientific articles, followed by Nigeria (11.4 per cent) and Kenya (6.6 per cent). These three countries alone produce two-thirds of total scientific output among sub-Saharan countries, thus implying a dark picture of scientific production in other countries (UNESCO 2010:285).
23. Sub-Saharan Africa's share of global patents is even more discouraging. At a continental level, including North African countries, the share only reaches 0.1 per cent of global scientifically based patents and inventions (UNESCO 2010:185). South Africa again stands out by accounting for more than two-thirds of the continent's registered patents.

Intimately linked to scientific production and invention and of direct pertinence to this study is the brain drain that is, mobility causing loss of skilled labour. With regard to PhD graduates, the lack of national research resources accompanied by aggressive marketing by public and private sectors in many OECD countries, offering attractive and well-paid employment, represent a major threat to the investment made in this small and strategic group. It has been suggested that many countries have lost more than 30 per cent of their labour force with tertiary qualifications through emigration to OECD countries.[24] For Cape Verde, Seychelles, Gambia, Ghana and Sierra Leone these losses range between 45 and 80 per cent (Hoba and Marfouk 2011:23).[25] Even if estimates of the brain drain from Africa are not yet sufficiently grounded in data, the few empirical studies that do exist suggest the problem is extensive and growing (Docquier and Marfouk 2006). Notwithstanding data deficiencies, brain drain has become a high priority in policy circles.[26] Above all there is consensus on the need for better data for monitoring the scope and impact of the brain drain: "[B]oth in Africa and Europe there still seems to be lack of awareness of the extent of brain drain and its impact at all levels, from academic to societal and economic" (European University Association 2010 cited in Hoba and Marfouk 2011:31).

The brain drain problem is associated with significant financial, institutional and societal costs. The outflow of skilled people, combined with growing demand in some areas, means that many African countries are forced to recruit expensive foreign personnel. This represents a double cost to society. It is estimated that today there are nearly 200,000 foreign experts in Africa, at a cost of US$ 4 billion per year. About 35 per cent of total ODA goes on salaries of imported skilled labour. Opposing the view that an outflow of skilled people is an irreversible loss to a society is a more recent strand in the literature arguing that this type of migration could help poor countries grow out of poverty more quickly than otherwise possible. One aspect of this argument is the role and impact of remittances. However, in relation to the position and role of the PhD graduate in society, the remittances argument may not outweigh the strategic

---

24. Many OECD countries now adjust their immigration policies and scholarships to increase retention rates: "There is wide agreement in Europe and North America that new initiatives to entice the 'best and brightest' of professionals from other countries, whom they educate, to stay and join the local labour force are a good idea. Efforts to liberalize visa regulations, open employment opportunities, permit postgraduate work, ease degree recognition, improve cooperation between universities, governments and industry, and many other initiatives are being implemented" (Altbach 2013).

25. Six of the ten countries with the highest proportion of skilled emigrants are in Africa, topped by Somalia. The statistics are unreliable, but it is estimated that one in six students trained at an African university leaves the continent, mainly for North America and Europe. According to United Nations Development Program Ethiopia lost almost 75 per cent of its skilled workforce between 1980 and 1990.

26. The AU, AAU and NEPAD have all recognised the importance of better information on the mobility of skilled individuals.

impact of having this small group of highly skilled individuals in place in their country of origin.

In conclusion, current global and African developments in higher education and research and in society at large have elements that potentially affect the career choices of PhD graduates. On a basic level, one may conclude that the premises of the competitive global knowledge economy, higher education being one, have increasingly challenged the connection between PhD training and research capacity at universities in many low-come countries, not least sub-Saharan countries. Of the factors discussed in this chapter, the following are the most prominent as regards mobility and career development among the sampled population: i) the gradually increased pressure on resources (budget and time-wise) for research at many national universities as a result of the current massi-fication in higher education (Altbach 2008), ii) increased policy-driven interna-tionalisation of research and higher education, leading to increased competition among and mobility within the international research community – the global hunt for highly skilled specialists (Kemal 2003); iii) the escalation of private, market-driven higher education institutions in many developing countries offer-ing limited or no research resources (Mamdani 2007); and iv) increased demand from other sectors of society, private and public, for PhD graduates to meet the demands of the global knowledge economy, such as institutional innovation capacity (Bloom 2005).

5.2 The development of research and higher education in Mozambique

As with many African sub-Saharan countries, higher education and research in Mozambique is a comparatively recent phenomenon, dating to 1962 with the creation of a branch (Estudos Gerais Universitários) of a Portuguese uni-versity, which six years later was upgraded to university status and renamed the University of Lourenco Margues (Chilundo 2002:4-6). In accordance with the elite-based rule generally applied by European colonial powers, access to higher education was largely restricted to Portuguese settlers. Consequently, until in-dependence in 1975, Mozambican students comprised less than 0.1 per cent of total higher education enrolment (Brito *et al.* 2008:304). There are no records of major research activity during the colonial period.

With Mozambique's independence in 1975 came radically new principles for higher education, which had to be reset from almost zero in terms of teaching resources. The prime role of the country's only higher learning institution, now renamed Eduardo Mondlane University, became educating skilled workers for the consolidation of independence and not least to offset the loss of trained staff in now abandoned positions in the country's administrative system. Notwith-standing the huge demand, the expansion of higher learning institutions was relatively slow and it was not until the mid-1980s that two new institutions were established.[27] This was followed by the country's first law on higher education in 1993, which confirmed the importance of tertiary education and opened the way for private enterprises.[28]

Persistent high demands from society for university-trained individuals coupled with the slow growth in the number of institutions and quality deficiencies, not least with regard to admissions and the mismatch with societal needs, prompted the government to launch two commissions, in 1997 and in 1999. The result was the Strategic Plan for Higher Education for 2000-2010 and the creation of the new Ministry for Higher Education, Science and Technology. In 2005, MHEST was split, with higher education being integrated into the Ministry of Education and Culture, while science and technology became part of a separate Ministry for Science and Technology. This division signalled the increased strategic significance afforded higher education and research as tools for development, but also gives rise to concerns about coordination between the two areas, not least in terms of recruitment of PhD candidates and dissemination of scientific results. It has been argued "the new arrangement seems to be based on the perception that higher education does not play a strong role in the science and innovation system but [is] rather merely a component of the national education system" (Brito *et al.* 2008:307).

The period from the mid-1990s to the present has been the most expansive in the history of higher education in Mozambique, both in terms of institutions and student enrolment. As Table 5.1 shows, the number of institutions has grown from four in 1995 to 18 in 2013.[29] A significant number of these new institutions are private enterprises, run on commercial lines. Private institutions now account for almost one-third of enrolled students. The most remarkable feature of higher education in the last 20 years is the dramatic increase in student enrolment, with almost four times as many students in 2013 as in 1995. Even though female student numbers have increased, disproportionality remains a problem, particularly at public institutions. In 2013, female students make up only 25 per cent of total enrolment at public institutions, while at private institutions

---

27. UP was established in 1985 to train teachers for the national education system, while ISRI was established in 1986 to train diplomatic staff.

28. The first three private institutions were established in 1996.

29. Eduardo Mondlane University (UEM), Universidade Pedagogica (UP), Universidade Catolica de Mozambique, Universidade Jean Peaget de Mozambique, Universidade Lurio, Universidad Poletecnica, Universidade Sao Tomas, Universidade Zambeze, Universidade Tecnica de Mozambique, Universidade Mussa Bin Bique, Instituto Superior de Ciencias de Saude, Instituto Superior Politecnica de Manica, Instituto de Superior de Ciencias e Tecnologicas de Mozambique, Instituto Superior de Transportes e Comunicacoes, Escola Superior de Economia e Gestao, Universidad Pedagogica Sagrade Familia, Instituto Superior de Ciencias e Tecnologia Aleberto Chipande, Instituto Superior Cristao, Instituto Superior Poletecnica de Gaza, Universidade Nautica de Mozambique and Universidade Jean Piaget de Mozambique

Table 5.1 Number of enrolled students and institutions by year (1975–2012)

Year	Student enrolment			Number of institutions		
	Public	*Private*	*Total*	*Public*	*Private*	*Total*
1975	2,433	0	2,433	1	0	1
1980	1,016	0	1,016	1	0	1
1985	1,442	0	1,442	2	0	2
1990	3,750	0	3,750	3	0	3
1995	6,890	0	6,890	4	0	4
2000	9,817	3,606	13,423	5	5	10
2004	15,113	7,143	22,256	6	6	12
2010	72,636	28,726	101 362	–	–	–
2011	79,333	33,454	112 787	8	13	21

Table appears in Brito et al. in Teffera and Knight 2008:307 and has been updated with figures for 2008 and 2012 (Source: Ministry of Education, Education Strategic Plan 2012–2016 and National Statistical Institute: Statistical yearbook 2012)

the share is 46 per cent. The skewed gender distribution has been explained by the more technical courses offered by public institutions (Ministry of Education and Culture in Teferra and Knight 2008).

The dramatic expansion in higher education over the last decade follows the pattern seen in other sub-Saharan countries, namely increased demand followed by expansive policy goals and instructions. Given similar preconditions, the challenges of expansion are to large extent the same as in other African countries. One important issue for this study is how expansion has affected conditions for research and career development among PhD graduates, who play a central role in the operation and quality of both research and training.[30]

In global terms, Mozambique is undoubtedly a very small provider of scientific knowledge. This has nothing to do with a lack of researchable areas, but is a direct consequence of the shortage of resources to support research and train researchers. With many years lost through the civil war, the country is currently one of the weakest research producers in sub-Saharan Africa. According to UNESCO statistics, the total number of researchers by 2010 was 337, or 16 researchers per million inhabitants. By comparison, South Africa, at the top of the list, has a total of 18,574 researchers or 382 researchers per million inhabitants (UNESCO 2010:284).[31] As in higher education generally, the low proportion of women in research (one-third of total researchers), particularly in the STEM sciences, is problematic.

---

30. According to government sources, total teaching staff in higher education increased from 1,500 in 2000 to almost 3,700 in 2004. Less than 25 per cent of these teachers are women. Full-time staff made up 32 per cent of the total. Of these, about 20 per cent had an MSc and only 13 per cent a PhD (MOSTIS 2006:6).

31. The meaning of "researcher" is not clear in UNESCO statistics, specifically whether it relates to staff members with a PhD degree. It is most likely the data also cover MSc graduates involved in research.

Most of the country's scientific production takes place at public universities (mainly at UEM, UP and ISRI) and in the 19 public scientific and technological research institutes (IICTs). As an indication of the degree of mobility among individuals that is the focus of this study, government documents claim that public universities employ around 80 per cent of those with PhD degrees (MOSTIS 2006: 4).

The national strategy for science, technology and innovation (MOSTIS) is central to understanding government policy objectives for research and provides the frame of priorities (research fields and human capacity building) within which PhD graduates orient themselves.[32] As regards research priority areas, the strategy adopts the same line of argument currently used by most other governments in Africa and worldwide, that is a focus on STEM sciences. Apart from education and health, the strategic research areas include energy, agriculture, mineral resources, water, marine science and fishing and construction. Notably, the social sciences and humanities are afforded a cross-cutting function in sustaining the strategic areas, along with such specific research areas as environmental sustainability, ethno-botany, gender equity and HIV/AIDS.

Of direct bearing on this study is the high priority given human resource development and the retention of highly skilled teaching and research staff. The strategy highlights the problem of competition for attractive employers outside the public education and research sector: "Management and administrative positions are often more lucrative than research posts, which acts as an incentive for many to leave active research" (MOSTIS 2006:25). Interestingly, this seems to be less of a problem among individuals holding PhDs. As has been shown, the government notes that the majority (80 per cent) of PhD graduates remain at universities. Probably due to the relative scarcity of highly skilled research staff, PhDs in particular, government policy does not reflect on the importance of also nurturing other sectors of society. To tackle the problem of retention, government argues for the need for increased international cooperation:

> [C]areers and in education and research may be made more attractive through [a] long-term program of collaboration with international universities and research institutions that offer opportunities for advanced study and research. This should include sabbatical programmes that encourage leading international researchers to spend their sabbaticals in Mozambican research institutions, thus allowing high-quality interaction between local researchers and their international colleagues. (MOSTIS 2006:25)

---

32. An interesting point is that the main goal of the strategy is to reduce poverty: the strategy "will enable the voices of the poorest sectors to be heard by the society, and science and technology will be used to give them the means to gain the upper hand against poverty." (MOSTIS 2006:14)

To further improve retention, the government also proposes the creation of centres of excellence. To meet demand for trained researchers in strategic research areas, an ambitious training plan has been formulated, with the goal of reaching 6,595 researchers by 2025 (660 in 2010, 2,638 by 2015 and 5,276 by 2020).[33] With only two years left to achieve the enormous jump projected for 2015 and a persistent shortage of qualified training and research staff, these goals seem rather over-optimistic.

33. The training plan has a fairly equal distribution among scientific disciplines, with a bias towards natural science (15 per cent), engineering and technology (20 per cent), medical sciences (20 per cent), agronomical sciences (20 per cent), social sciences (12.5 per cent) and the humanities (12.5 per cent). It is not clear whether the human resource development plan aims at the training of only PhD graduates, or if other degrees qualify for the "researcher" designation.

6. International donor support for PhD training: Situating Swedish bilateral support for research capacity-building in Mozambique

Quite a few international donors have a long record of supporting capacity building at research institutions in Africa, many with PhD training as a central component. There are, however, significant differences among donors in terms of scope, design and ownership of these programs, arising from different views on how institutional capacity building should be achieved (ODI 2007). The principal rationale behind Swedish support has been that each country should have at least one university capable of being a resource for the establishment and expansion of national research and higher education. In keeping with this approach, the training of PhD graduates (using a sandwich program designed to sustain links with the home institution) constitutes a core component in achieving the capacity to formulate and conduct research of high quality and relevance. The sandwich approach is believed to promote capacity-building efforts more holistically, moving beyond the individual researcher, by gradually transferring responsibilities, administratively and substantively, from the Swedish counterpart to the partner in the collaborating country. Hence, one important milestone in this approach is the establishment of local PhD programs.

Swedish development support to Mozambique dates back to the mid-1970s and follows on the political support for the independence struggle led by Frelimo. Research cooperation began a few years later, in 1978, in the form of support to the sole higher learning institution in the country, UEM, at the time severely affected by an extensive loss of staff. Since the late 1980s, the support has mainly targeted capacity building though training in accordance with the sandwich model, and university-wide research infrastructure such as ICT, library, administration and management (Sida 2003:20). As displayed in Table 6.1, with few exceptions the support to UEM has increased steadily, making Sida one of the main external supporters of research there.

Following the sandwich model of PhD training, most candidates have since inception been registered at Swedish institutions and since the late 1990s increasingly also in South African institutions. Consequently, they have also defended their theses at these places. According to the principal idea of the sandwich model, candidates should over the course of their training alternate between home institution and external institution, the frequency being variable, depending on individual needs. An important aspect of the program is that candidates

Table 6.1 Swedish support to UEM per period of agreement (in SEK '000)

Years	1978–80	1981–85	1986–90	1991–94	1995–97	1998–2000	2001–05	2006–10	2011–15
Total	1,395	11,765	29,070	44,300	28,669	79,178	84,133	175,555	195,000

Source: Sida 2003

should undertake research in the home institution, leading to the building of a research culture. Earlier in the Mozambican program, the implementation of this approach was criticised. A Sida evaluation in 2003 concluded that "most of the training programmes under the Sida/SAREC cannot be classified as Sandwich type, since the candidates return only to teach or to do administrative work and not least attending to other job commitments to secure an adequate income. Too little time is spent on research at home" (Sida 2003:22). This problem is not unique to Mozambique and is apparent in most of Sida's bilateral research programs. Nevertheless, it ties in with the critical question of how training programs of this type evolve over time in terms of building local research capacity and what kind of incentives for mobility and career development they produce. All the PhD graduates in this study have worked within the sandwich model, but as will be shown their stories and experiences differ significantly.

Swedish development support for research has long been committed to the idea that PhD training is the main foundation for building research capacity.[34] In most collaborating countries, current and past, the approach has consumed a major part of the resources allocated to bilateral research cooperation. Over the years, confidence in the model seems to have been so high that it has overshadowed the need to examine the long-term effects of such support: what is the function and impact on mobility and career development of this resource-intensive investment in single individuals and how has this approach evolved over time? Despite more than 30 years of support for PhD training in Mozambique and other countries, only one tracing study (of Vietnam) has been conducted (Sida 2009). In the case of Mozambique, it has been concluded "there are no systematic records on Ph.D. and M.Sc. graduates with Sida/SAREC funding, neither at UEM nor at Sida/SAREC. Moreover, there are no tracer studies and it is next to impossible to estimate to what extent these graduates remain at UEM" (Sida 2003).

---

34. The importance of support for PhD training is clearly stated in the Swedish government's policy and strategy for research in Swedish development cooperation, 2010–14 (Swedish Government 2010).

7. Results

The results are presented around two main themes, each with several sub-themes.

1) *Organisation of and experiences during PhD training.* From this theme, three sub-themes follow: i) individual preconditions and organisational set-up of training; ii) experiences of the training situation iii) experiences of discrimination during training

2) *Career development and mobility after graduation.* From this second theme, three sub-themes follows: i) individual preconditions and organisational set-up of training for past and current positions; ii) working conditions; and iii) mobility since graduation.

Separate analysis is provided for those who have already finished PhD training (graduates) and those still in training (candidates).

7.1 Theme I: Organisation of and experiences during PhD training

Under this theme, the results relating to individual preconditions and organisational set-up of training will be displayed and analysed (e.g., position and age upon commencing training, type of dissertation and country of training). This is followed by examination of type of dissertation and respondents' experiences of the training, with particular focus on areas of dissatisfaction (e.g., supervision and research resources in the country of training and in Mozambique). Special attention is given to the experience of discrimination during the period of training. Finally, results relating to aspects of mobility during the period of training will be displayed and analysed (e.g., stay rates in country of training versus home country, practical arrangements and the implications of these).

7.1.1 Individual preconditions and organisational set-up of training

The great majority of respondents (96 per cent) reported that their training was organised in accordance with the sandwich model. All those few who reported other types of training modality referred to full-time study in a foreign institution. No full-time studies were reported among those registered for training after 1997. However, as will be shown elsewhere, the sandwich modality displays great elasticity in terms of stay rates, both in total and in average duration of each stay. The sandwich model has never included directives specifying duration of stay in the foreign institution. This is basically sound, but in each case a point may be reached when too long stay rates in the foreign institution may be counterproductive for the home institution, both in terms of supporting the status quo and more importantly in building a research capacity and culture, the modality's guiding p rinciple.

Since UEM has been the sole focus of Swedish-Mozambican research cooperation, the great majority (98 per cent) of the responding PhD graduates/candidates originate there.[35] A similar percentage applies to the position of the graduates/candidates at the time of starting training, with more than 94 per cent holding a staff position at UEM. The remaining 6 per cent were postgraduate students at the time of recruitment. The findings confirm the picture regarding entry into PhD training in most of Sida's bilateral research training programs, indicating that the educational level of staff members is still not sufficient to allow for the "external" intake of candidates for postgraduate programs.

Linked to the prerequisites for recruitment is the question of age when starting PhD training. Although this issue is not supported by any studies, it has been the subject of discussion in many Sida-funded research training programs and criticism has been raised about the selection of relatively old candidates as a result of formal and informal seniority rules in collaborating institutions.

In the recruitment of the Mozambican candidates in this study, the presence of this age bias seems to be comparatively low, though with a few noteworthy observations. As shown in Table 7.1, a majority of respondents started their training before the age of 41. There is, however, significant variation in the representation of women and men in the three age categories between 25 and 40. Men seem to start their training earlier than women, with a high representation of men (51 per cent) in first two age categories, while a majority of women were found in the third category. In addition, a significantly higher proportion of women started their training between 41 and 45 (32 per cent). The equivalent proportion for men was found in the age category 25 to 30. Supporting the perception of old age bias in recruitment for PhD training is the proportion of men (23 per cent) in the two upper age categories 46-50 and 51-55. However, by cross-checking these figures with year of training commencement, it appears that the great majority of older candidates stem from early years under investigation, that is the early 1990s. Generally, the results indicate a tendency towards earlier commencement, regardless of gender, as one moves along the time line. Still, there was a significant difference between women and men as regards age when starting PhD training.

Table 7.1 Age when starting PhDs by gender in per cent (N)

Age/ Gender	25–30	31–35	36–40	41–45	46–50	51–55	Total
Female	3.2% (1)	6.4% (2)	51.6% (16)	32.2% (10)	6.4% (2)	0 (0)	100% (31)
Male	21.6% (11)	33.3% (17)	15.7% (8)	7.8% (4)	15.7% (8)	5.9% (3)	100% (51)
Total	14.6% (12)	23.2% (19)	29.3% (24)	17.1% (14)	12.2% (10)	3.6% (3)	100% (82)

---

35. According to information in available registers and records, the figure is also representative of the total sampled population. In cases where respondents specified other institutions, all have close cooperation with UEM, e.g., the National Institute of Meteorology.

Type of dissertation

In international academia there is general tendency towards the article-based dissertation at the expense of the monograph. The survey results indicate that this tendency seems to apply to the surveyed Mozambican graduates and candidates. As indicated in Table 7.2, article-form dissertations have over the period of investigation become the dominant form in most disciplines, irrespective of country of graduation, with the social sciences and humanities being the exception.[36] The proportion of article-based dissertations also increases as one moves along the time line of investigation, including in the social sciences and humanities. Not displayed in the table are candidates still in training, but results for this category seem to reinforce the picture of progressive movement towards dissertation by articles.

Table 7.2. Type of dissertation by country and discipline (N)

	Sweden					South Africa					Total
	Sci	Med/Vet	Soc/Hum	Tech	Agri	Sci	Med/Vet	Soc/Hum	Tech	Agri	
Mono-graph	11.8% (2) 25.0%	11.8% (2) 28.6%)	23.5% (4) 66.6%	5.9% (1) 25.0%	17.6% (3) 50.0%	0% (0) 0%	0% (0) 0%	11.8% (2) 100%	5.9% (1) 25.0%	0% (0) 0%	100% (17)
Article	20.7% (6) 75.0%	17.2% (5) 71.4%	6.9% (2) 33.3%	10.3% (3) 75.0%	10.3% (3) 50.0%	13.8% (4) 100%	10.3% (3) 100%	0% (0) 0%	10.3% (3) 75.0%	6.9% (2) 100%	100% (29)
Total	100% (8)	100% (7)	100% (6)	100% (4)	100% (6)	100% (4)	100% (3)	100% (2)	100% (4)	100% (2)	N: 46

The table covers only respondents who have graduated. The upper percentage for type of dissertation refers to the proportion between countries and disciplines, while the lower percentage refers to proportion of type of dissertation in a specific discipline in Sweden and South Africa.

Judging from respondents' narratives, the preference for dissertation by article seems to be not only the expression of a general trend in academia, but also a deliberate feature of the sandwich model. Several respondents asserted that the article form was more compatible with the mobile character of sandwich model, allowing for distinct checkpoints as one moved ahead with the research. In some cases, the choice of type of dissertation had not been optional, with dissertation by article being presented by the training institution as the only alternative. The following narratives elaborate on this:

> For me the article form was the only option and my supervisor made it clear to me already at the beginning. Since most people in my field write dissertation by articles I didn't even consider writing a monograph. Now when looking back I realise that the article form was very suitable for the way the

---

36. These are also the exceptions internationally.

training was organised, going back and forth between Sweden and home. It allowed me to set up milestones and keep close contact with my supervisor. (female)

I had colleagues doing their training in Sweden and in South Africa who both wrote monographs and I saw the difficulties they were facing, particularly the supervision. If the supervision is both far away and poor, you run a great risk to fail in the end. I have seen it happen, you put a lot of effort into something for a long time and if you are on the wrong track from the beginning it will end by catastrophe. Therefore for me dissertation by articles seemed to be a more secure way of training and it worked very well for me.
(male)

7.1.2 Experiences of the training situation

The experience of PhD training varied significantly according to academic discipline. Graduates in social sciences, humanities and medicine display greater dissatisfaction across most variables, particularly with regard to supervision in the country of training, co-supervision and research training in the country of training. On the other hand, and not surprisingly, social science and humanities graduates showed the lowest rates of dissatisfaction regarding research resources in Mozambique. Science, medicine and technology scored high on this variable. Graduates in agricultural science and technology generally displayed the lowest levels of dissatisfaction. No significant discrepancy was apparent when controlling for period of time. The results from controlling for candidates in different disciplines did reveal significant differences, but the pattern remained largely intact.

Mobility in relation to the training situation

The experiences of the sandwich program have also been analysed in terms of stay rates[37] in the country of training and academic discipline. The results indicate a slight tendency towards longer total stay rates among graduates that pursued their training in South Africa compared to graduates trained in Sweden. Controlling for average time of stay, the South African group represented a significantly higher share among those reporting shorter average stays, which indicates a more frequent exchange in terms of visits.

The distribution of stays in country of training in relation to academic field revealed no significant variation (also when controlling for gender or country of training). The need for scientific resources such as laboratories and technical equipment in the STEM sciences seems not to have led to longer stays among graduates in these disciplines compared to graduates in the social sciences and humanities, who reported the lowest dissatisfaction with existing research re-

---

37. Stay rate refers to length and frequency of stays in the country of training during.

Polar 7.1 PhD graduates' average stay in country of training by country of training in per cent

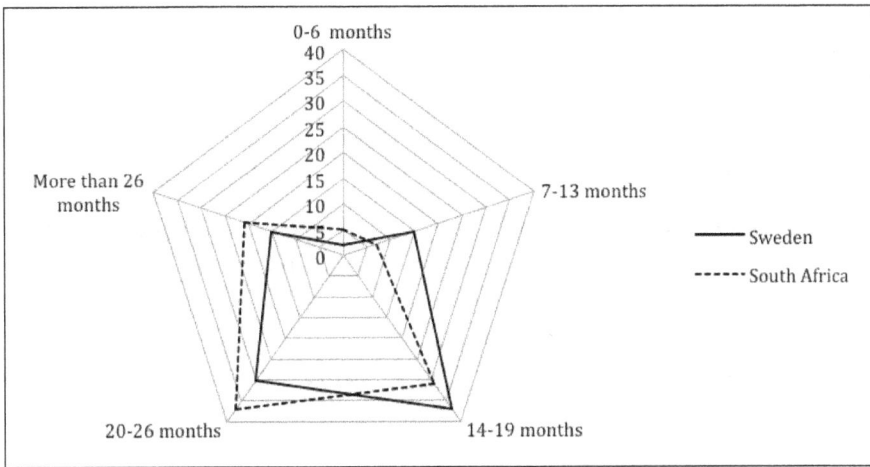

sources at UEM. Even though access to laboratories and equipment was a strong motive for stays in the country of training, particularly in Sciences, Technology, Engineering and Mathematics –the STEM sciences, the main explanation given by respondents was to get away from time-consuming teaching and administrative work at the home university in order to focus exclusively on PhD research.

I had no time to dedicate to my PhD research when I was in Mozambique. The stays in Sweden really made me focus on the PhD work because there was nothing else around. I was away from my family, so even the weekends became workdays. It was really hectic and very constructive, but also very hard and lonesome. (woman)

During the period of training in Mozambique you had a lot of lectures and administrative works that subtract the amount of time available for research. Basically it was very hard to focus on the PhD research while at UEM. The time I was in South Africa I did 90 per cent of my dissertation work. (man)

Reportedly, respondents (graduates and candidates) ascribed high importance to the sandwich model's inherent mobility. However, in looking at how this was expressed, the positive features of the mobility in the program seem largely to relate to the opportunity to go abroad for training and not so much to the model's principal objective –simultaneously building research capacity and culture at the home university. According to respondents, the heavy teaching and administrative load at the university has served as an effective barrier to the emergence of a research culture in all academic areas, both during training and after graduation.

> For me it was impossible to simultaneously engage in my own training and build up a research capacity at my department when everything moved in the opposite direction, with more and more students and teaching. (woman

> Whenever in Mozambique the motion was very slow because the structure was not helpful. It was difficult to perform the assignment due to lack of support at home. (man)

Generally, female and male respondents were positive about the mobility aspect of the sandwich model. According to respondents, the design of the program gave the opportunity to keep an open mind about different contexts, to see taken-for-granted aspects and to broaden international networks. Another positive dimension brought up was the possibility to stay in contact with home countries in various areas:

> The sandwich program allows staying open-minded. You see things differently when you change contexts. This is what I try to give to my students too – you need to change perspectives. (man)

> A sandwich model, to me, it is always very good in the past, in the present and probably in the future. Because you never lose the links to your country, what is going on in the country, with your family. (woman)

> It provided me with opportunity of practically testing my theoretical background on the subject matter by engaging hands-on with my practical fieldwork. Coming back from the field I was always loaded with concrete ground issues to theoretically engage with my supervisor and other professors, who I was regularly interacting with. (man)

However, both female and male respondents remarked that in practice the sandwich model didn't work equally for women and men, and this may necessitate different incentives for women to apply for the program. A full account of the reasons for low overall participation by women in the program would involve a different study, one taking historical and geopolitical structures into account, and the intent here is much more limited. It is to analyse how women and men talk about their experiences of mobility while in the program. Particular emphasis is given to challenges to mobility, since this yields information on how attractive the model appears to women and men. This will be further developed in the following.

The program at the intersection of gender, age and family situation
In the interviews, no man or woman mentioned knowing any men who had refrained from applying to the program because of their role as fathers. In this context, the interviews and survey reveal that men seemed to enter the PhD program regardless of number or age of children. By contrast, both women and

men stated that the program's requirement for mobility was one of the main factors preventing particularly young women with children from participating, and that they knew of several women who had refrained from applying because of their caring responsibilities as mothers.

> I know that some women would like to go and participate in a sandwich program but they have difficulties with their partners, they don't allow them. And sometimes it is difficult for them to go because of kids, yes, things like that. (woman, social)

> When there are kids in the game the things become complicated. Because when the husband is away, it means that all the work is on the woman. Imagine the opposite, the man with kids [...] this means that the woman will not leave until she is old. (man)

There were also clear gender differences regarding how the sandwich model was lived in practice. This was exemplified by analysing how women and men talk about how long they could stay and would have liked to stay in the country of training (Polar 7.2). While men spent longer periods away from Mozambique, women tended to go back and forth for shorter periods. As shown in Polar 7.3 there is a significant difference in men's and women's average stays in the country of training. The great majority of women (almost half the respondents) had an average stay of two to three months. Close to 75 per cent of women reported an average stay ranging from two to five months. The distribution of time periods for men displayed a more even picture, but with a significant orientation towards longer average stays in country of training.

Polar 7.2 PhD graduates' total stay in country of training by gender in per cent

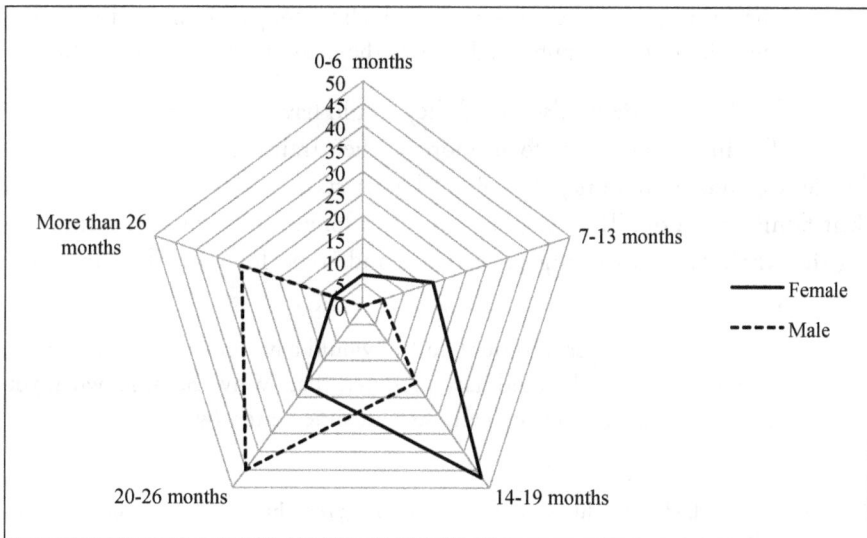

Polar 7.3 PhD graduates' average stay in country of training by gender in per cent

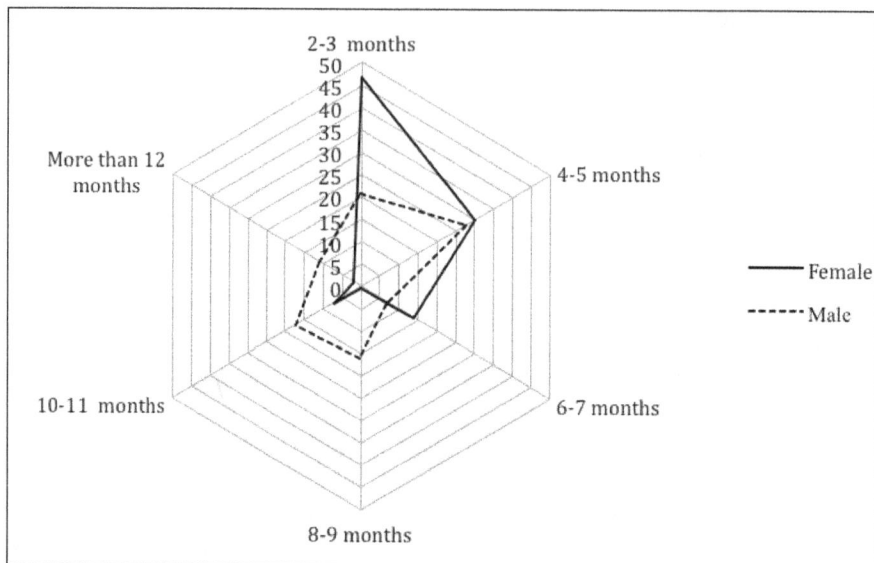

Reportedly, moving back and forth between locations caused difficulties in getting involved in host department activities. In this vein, several male respondents pointed out that long periods away from Mozambique were particularly important in being able to focus entirely on research, have access to regular supervision and other scientific facilities such as laboratories, library, etc.

> The first 3 year period I stayed in Sweden during 3-6 months to do course work and discuss my fieldwork with my supervisor [...]The following years I stayed in Sweden almost three full years. Full-time. Because my supervisor felt that I needed to make more progress. Since I had my data it was good that I stayed these three years, I could publish papers which where part from my thesis. So I used these three years to publish. This was the main work of my thesis. (man)

Several female respondents also noted they would have liked longer stays in the county of training in order to focus more on their training and research. When female respondents were negative about longer stays, it was mainly because of their family situation. They emphasised that a longer stay would require moving the whole family, causing uncertainty and stress for both their men and children.[38]

> Yes, if I had been younger, without family, I would have preferred to stay longer, to bring my family. Yes I would have preferred that. Why? Because, when you are there for a longer period you can use your time better. (woman)

---

38. Only one man had moved his whole family, indicating that this was not very common practice for men either.

But there were also differences among the women. The women who had participated in the program particularly mentioned that they were beyond the age of having small kids and that this was a main factor allowing them to leave their families behind and join the program. From the viewpoint of age, they had previously been too young to be able to join the program.

In this vein, many respondents referred to a recent Sida policy limiting the age for entering PhD training to 40 years. This policy was mentioned as a new barrier for women applicants for the PhD program. To what extent the policy has been institutionalised and how it is put into practice in different subject areas is not known. What is known is that one respondent reported that two of his female colleagues were denied access to the program because they were considered too old. This indicates the need for further research on the degree of implementation of the age policy and its consequences for gender equality more broadly, that is how gender, family situation and age relations intersect and create differing conditions for participation in research and mobility.

While the interviews shed light on the differences among women, the interviews also indicate that responsibility for participating and succeeding within the program is largely placed on women. This not only leaves men's positions and responsibility unproblematised, but also tends to individualise the problems women may encounter. Therefore more research on the institutional structures enhancing and/or preventing gender equality in sandwich programs is needed.

Experiences of resources for research and supervision
The results from the survey indicate that women researchers experienced more dissatisfaction than men regarding supervision and co-supervision. This supports previous research from the Global North indicating that it is particularly in informal academic situations, such as supervision, that women experience exclusion and discrimination (Caplan 1994, Morley 1999) and that these processes are often subtle and difficult to grasp (Husu 2001, Mählck 2003). As displayed in Polar 7.4, resources for research and co-supervision in Mozambique clearly stand out as the dominant problem experienced by respondents. In both these areas, women seem to have experienced a somewhat higher degree of dissatisfaction. When cross-checking with period of training, the picture seems also to have persisted over time, with few variations between graduates from the early1990s and more recently.

Compared with PhD candidates in training at the time of the survey, some minor, though interesting, changes in pattern can be observed.[39] There seems to be a somewhat higher level of dissatisfaction with Swedish supervision com-

---

39. PhD candidates in training are included to provide information on the current situation. This is important for assessing proceedings over time, not least with regard to capacity building.

Polar 7.4 Percentage of PhD graduates dissatisfied with their period of training by gender and reason for dissatisfaction

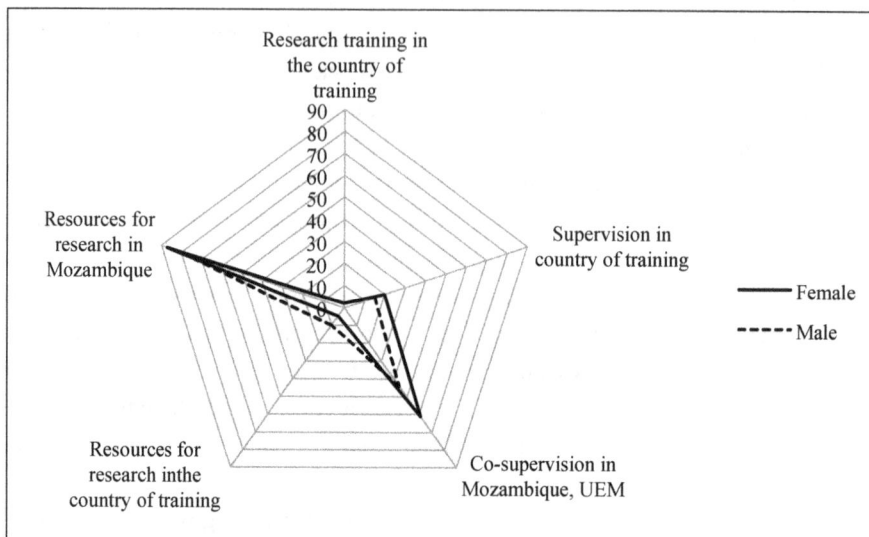

pared to the results of the graduated population, particularly among women. Further, the level of dissatisfaction with resources in Mozambique continues to show no significant difference between women and men. This also applies to the conditions of co-supervision in Mozambique. In Mozambique, such difficulties related to access to necessary infrastructure (particularly in the natural sciences and engineering) as well as to finding time to focus on research, as candidates were caught up with other tasks such as teaching and supervision. Some women interviewees suggested these processes were highly gendered, indicating that men through their male networks could arrange better working conditions during their PhD training periods in Mozambique than women. Sometimes, responsibility for extended family was also mentioned as negatively impacting the time for academic work.

When cross-checking level of satisfaction by country of training, the survey results revealed a somewhat different picture for different countries. As shown in Polar 7.5, graduates trained in South Africa generally seem to have experienced greater dissatisfaction compared to their Swedish equivalents. Particularly high levels of dissatisfaction among South African graduates seem to relate to supervision and research training (mainly coursework activities). No significant variations were observed when cross-checking with time of graduation.

The results on candidates in the two countries, shows a similar pattern to Polar 7.5 on graduates, but with a few notable changes. To some extent, levels of dissatisfaction with research training and supervision among the candidates in Sweden seem to have increased.

Polar 7.5 Percentage of PhD graduates dissatisfied with their period of training by country of training and reason for dissatisfaction

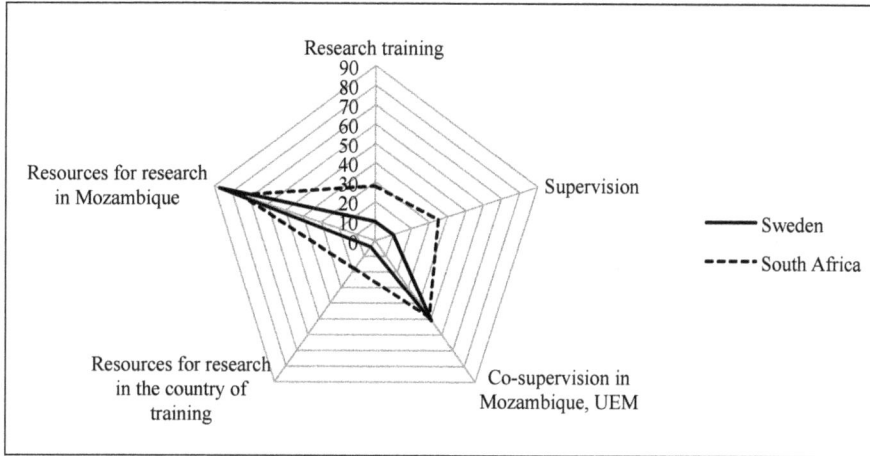

7.1.3 Experience of discrimination during training[40]

In the survey, special attention was given to the experience of discrimination during the period of training, both in the country of training and while at the institution in Mozambique. In addition to the factors displayed in the above result compilations, which are more absolute in character, different forms of discrimination during training are believed to influence the experience, performance and outcome.

The results indicate discrimination in some areas, notably relating to family situation and position at workplace. Women seem to have experienced discrimination in relation to family situation to a significantly greater extent than men. This result links to divisions, much referred to by respondents, in responsibility in Mozambican society whereby women often have chief responsibility for children and household. It would seem that family situation does not exist as a basis for possible discrimination against men.[41]

---

40. The definitional frames for discrimination range from unwanted attention to direct harassment. Respondents were asked to rate their experience of discrimination in relation to categories ranging from not at all to a very large extent. In this study gender, age, ethnic background, socioeconomic background (class), skin colour, sexual orientation, disability, position at workplace and family situation formed the basis for classifying discrimination. The experience of discrimination is specifically limited to the academic workplace, that is UEM. In compiling the results, the analytical focus has been on the two upper response options for experiencing discrimination, to a large and a very large extent. The results for graduate and candidate respondents have been merged.

41. Low figures for disability, socioeconomic background, skin colour and sexual orientation do not necessarily preclude discrimination on these grounds, but this may take more subtle and untraceable form, or the grounds may never surface, e.g., sexual orientation, and give rise to discrimination.

Polar 7.6 Percentage of PhD graduates/candidates experiencing discrimination at UEM by gender and reason for discrimination

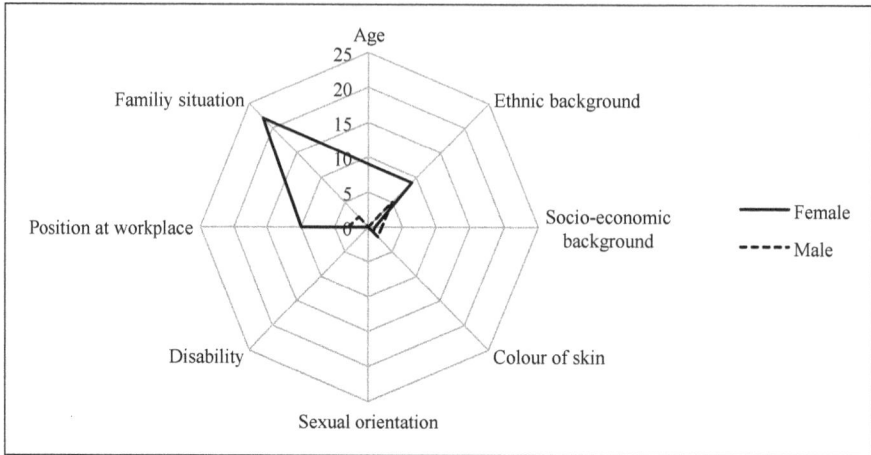

In contrast to the results revealed by the survey, very few researchers, when directly asked "have you experienced discrimination or negative treatment in your career?" in interviews, would agree with the proposition. The difficulties with researching negative treatment and/or discrimination in academia are well documented, the fear of "becoming the problem" is often mentioned as a main explanatory factor for the reluctance to talk about negative treatment and/or discrimination (Caplan 1994, Husu 2000, Mählck 2003). Therefore follow-up questions on the respondents everyday work life and opinion of gender equality and equity in Academia more broadly was also posed. From these broader themes experiences of negative treatment and/or discrimination could be analysed. In the context of this research, additional factors such as the limited number of research-intensive higher education institutions and PhDs in Mozambique, may add to the picture. Moreover, the nature of the project, being commissioned research and the overall link to Sida, may have contributed to reluctance to talk about obstacles in relation to careers. Finally, there is a need to acknowledge the problematic dimension of this type of project, which could easily lead to reproduction of postcolonial knowledge relations. From this perspective, reluctance to answer certain questions in interviews could also be read as acts of resistance. These methodological considerations will require much more attention in future research.

Accounts of discrimination would instead come up in relation to other topics, which have been mentioned previously, such as conditions for academic careers, mobility or more generally in relation to everyday work experiences. The following section will look deeper into the experiences of everyday research and experiences of supervision and resources in the different workplaces in Mozambique, Sweden or South Africa.

Experiences of discrimination in relation to supervision and resources
In Mozambique the dominant overall theme that emerged was the uneven distribution of caring responsibilities, which prevented women from reaching top academic positions. Both women and men emphasised this. The second most frequent discriminatory theme was the presence of old-boy networks.

> Yes, here in Mozambique you know, women would never leave their kids, they would never leave the household to be taken care of by the man, no that would never happen. Therefore it is more difficult for a woman to go to university, to do research. (male)

> No, I have never experienced discrimination, I'm a very strong woman and I have had good support, but I know others who has, yes [...] of course there has been ... incidents... like when this senior male academic tried to diminish my research publically. (woman)

> I always worked alone in my subject, and now, all new recruits are in a different field than me.
> – The new recruits, are they women or men?
> – They are all men, in the same field as the male researcher leader. I ask why? Why is this? How will I be able to do research, to build up my subject area if I'm alone all the time? (woman)

In Sweden and South Africa discrimination was displayed through workplace cultures and in the supervision relation. Most respondents had positive overall experiences of supervision and training resources in Sweden. However, within these narratives instances of not being able to enter into departmental activities as well as general feelings of isolation were persistent. As such, experience in Sweden points to more subtle forms of exclusion compared to South Africa. Here reference was made to language limitations as well as cultural differences. For example, several respondents mentioned they were not greeted in the corridor or approached during lunch or coffee breaks. As the micro-politics analytical framework reveals, there are many ways of producing exclusion, silence and isolation being among the most effective (Morley 1999).

The experience of isolation seems to have been less difficult where the department had a significant number of international students who could form a mutual support group. At the same time, such departments were more likely to have built up a support infrastructure for international students. A woman researcher emphasised the international character of the Swedish department, with many international students, as contributing to her positive experience of the PhD training period and her stay in Sweden. To what extent this created opportunities for international students to mingle, or meant that international students could access key departmental personnel, is an issue still to be researched.

In South Africa, the experiences had a different slant. Many respondents indicated they had chosen South Africa because of its geographical proximity, which allowed them to travel to and from Mozambique more easily. However, being in South Africa had not been as easy as expected.

> I got my PhD because of my local supervisor here, she was always there for me, but in South Africa I had to go chasing after my supervisor: please read this and time goes and sometimes you have to move on and work with the chapters and he still has not read it. [...] it was a difficult time there, with the administration, they would not tell you things. When I needed to get access to a computer they would say that they didn't have any. I mean this is a research institution, people work with computers (woman)

> South Africa is a very brutal country. Being in South Africa was not easy, being a black man. Doing a PhD in South Africa is very hard. I know several who has been delayed quite a bit. (man)

> Supervision during my time in South Africa was difficult. I didn't know what to expect nor the rights I had as a PhD candidate [...] I was delayed quite a bit because I was not given a supervisor and when I got one he was not very familiar with my topic. I had a feeling of being last in line all through my training, because South African professors give first priority to local candidates or candidates doing research in that professor's own project or research area. (women)

Negative treatment by the supervisor and/or other staff was emphasised in the interviews. The respondents related this to the legacy of apartheid and intensifying xenophobia in South Africa, but also to more subtle expressions of discrimination within academia. The sample narratives above come from respondents' everyday academic lives, such as problems with accessing supervision and computer infrastructure and lack of administrative information. Respondents suggested that, taken together, these events seriously delayed their PhD training and finalisation. These results indicate the importance of everyday work events for the outcome of an academic career and support previous research in the global north (see also Cole & Singer 1991).

Discrimination and isolation at the intersection of gender, academic position, nationality skin-colour and university context

When controlling for country of training (Polar 7.7) graduates and candidates who had trained or were training at South African universities accounted for the larger share of those reporting discrimination on the basis of nationality and skin colour. Also notable is the comparatively high proportion of respondents trained in Sweden with experiences of discrimination on the basis of skin colour. While the numbers may not be extremely high, the results are nevertheless interesting. Sweden and South Africa are often described as polar opposites in dominant discourses on democracy and discrimination. Therefore the similari-

Polar 7.7 Percentage of PhD graduates/candidates experiencing discrimination while in country of training by country of training and reason for discrimination

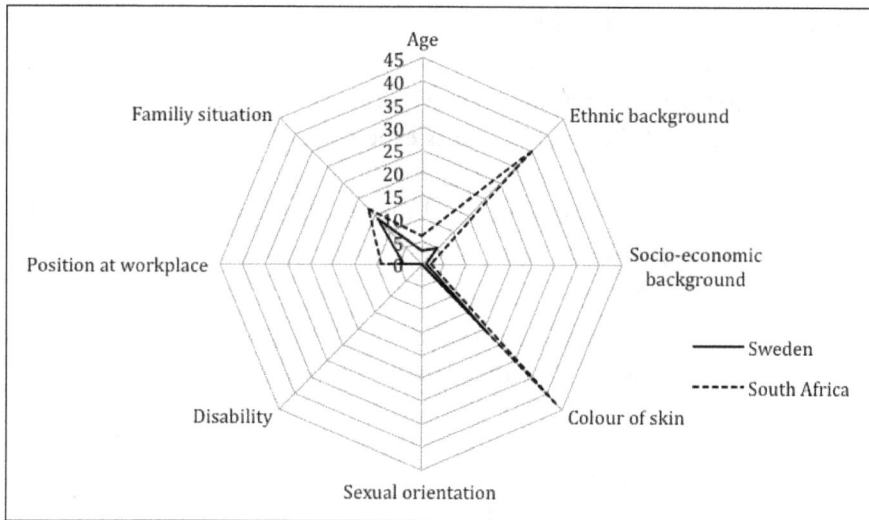

ties in discrimination patterns regarding skin colour are noteworthy insofar as they challenge and provide a basis for formulating new research questions. The patterns of discrimination displayed in the preceding two polars seem also to have been persistent over time. Further, the results did not show significant variation in rates of discrimination among academic disciplines.

The following quotations relate to experiences of discrimination based on intersections of skin-colour, nationality, academic postion and gender. The experiences also differ between the different university contexts (Sweden and South Africa).

> The issue of apartheid still has consequences today. I was a Mozambican, you know a foreigner, but at the same time a black woman. And all this issues and doing a PhD, because if I had been doing an honours degree or master's degree, people don't mind. But when you are in a PhD program they make your life difficult ... I'm not sure how to say it ... being in South Africa is not easy. Being a black woman in South Africa, they will make your life a hell! [...] I got funds from abroad but I didn't receive my funding. Somebody took them.
> – Took them? Here at this university?
> – No there, in South Africa. Somebody took them or gave them to somebody else. This is what I'm saying. It is tough to study in South Africa. (woman)

While recognising that the legacy of apartheid still made academic life difficult for black staff in South Africa, a black male researcher talked about how intersections of skin-colour and nationality created different conditions for him as compared to other black staff members at a South African university. As a black man, he had felt the expectation to talk in one of the local languages, since English was seen as the language of the oppressor. With his black skin and broken English, he had felt he didn't have access to his white colleagues, and since he didn't speak any local language, he was not included in the community of black colleagues. Everyday life outside the university had also been difficult, making him feel isolated, and he had sometimes experienced hostility just by walking on the streets.

The narratives of graduates who had undergone PhD training in Sweden revolved around a general feeling of isolation ranging from not being noticed to having felt unwelcome.

> Sweden is a particular place, after a while I learned not to take it personally, that people didn't greet me in the corridor, or looked at me in the coffee room. (man)

> You see, there are two kinds of swedes, those who have been abroad and those who have never been abroad. The first group made me feel very welcome, but the other group. Oh they ignored me, made me feel like a thing (woman)

While the incidents from Sweden were seldom discussed in terms of skin colour, they are nevertheless interesting to relate to the results of the survey, in which perceived discrimination based on skin colour is pronounced. Taken together, the survey and interview results support previous research in Sweden on the significance of a white body for the likelihood of being considered a good researcher, while researchers with non-white bodies were more vulnerable to existing structures of inequality, such as requirements for speaking Swedish, etc. (Mählck 2013). Research from South Africa indicates that race still shapes an academic's career prospects and that black women are particularly vulnerable to these tendencies (Mabokela & Magubane 2004). In this context, this result calls for future intersectional sensitive research into how inequality is produced in transnational academic labour in different university contexts (See also Anthias 2012 for a discussion of intersectional research on inequality in transnational work relations).

7.2 Theme II: Career development and mobility after graduation
Under this heading, the results relating to the individual development of graduates will be set out and analysed. These results fall under four sub-themes: current positions and working conditions; research output and collaboration; geographical mobility; and sectoral mobility.

7.2.1 Current employment positions and working conditions
The survey results indicate a significant correlation between fields of employment and the overall objective of PhD training, i.e., building research capacity

Diagram 7.1 Percentage of graduates per type of position

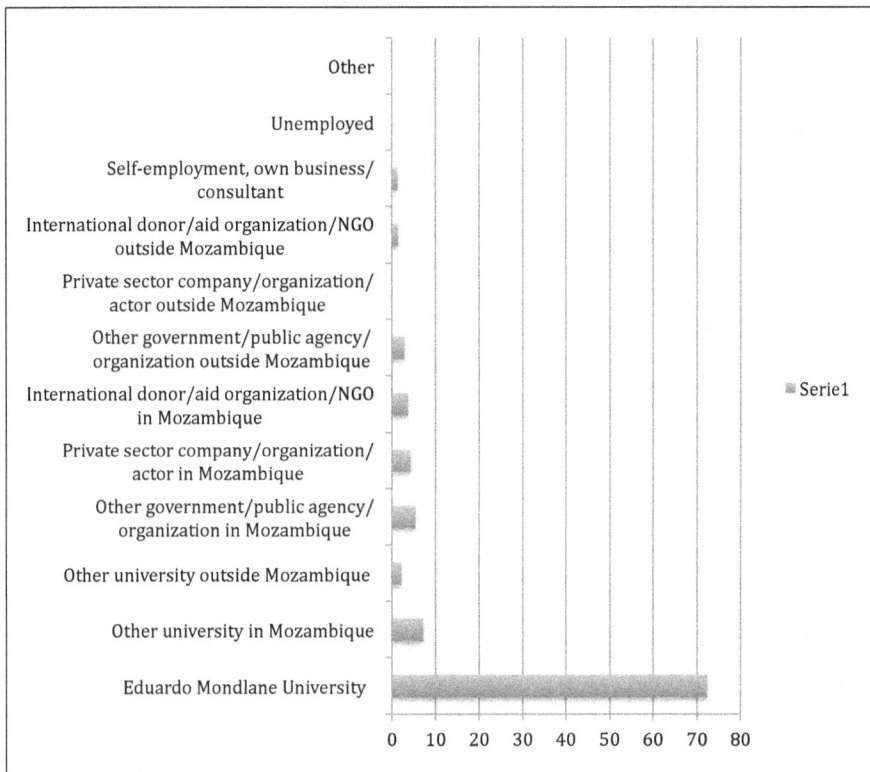

at the university. As shown in Diagram 7.1, the great majority (72 per cent) of those graduating after 1990 were employed at UEM in 2012. Despite a decade of rapid expansion of higher education institutions, only a small proportion (7.1 per cent) of responding graduates are employed by other universities in the country. Notably, the generally higher salaries paid by the expanding market-driven private universities seem not to have influenced the choice of workplace among those graduates still in the academic sector. Outside academia, other government or public actors and private companies in Mozambique have constituted alternative employment markets for PhD graduates, but only to a small extent (less than 10 per cent). Employment options outside Mozambique (both in academia and other sectors) have attracted only about 6 per cent of graduates, indicating a quite small degree of geographical mobility. When controlling for gender, only minor changes in the distribution of employment position emerged. Women tend to have an even stronger preference for staying at UEM, at the expense of their representation in all other employment categories. No significant variation was found among graduates from different academic disciplines.

The distribution of positions among responding graduates contained some interesting, though not surprising, elements (Diagram 7.2). On the whole, quite

Diagram 7.2 Percentage of graduates per position by gender

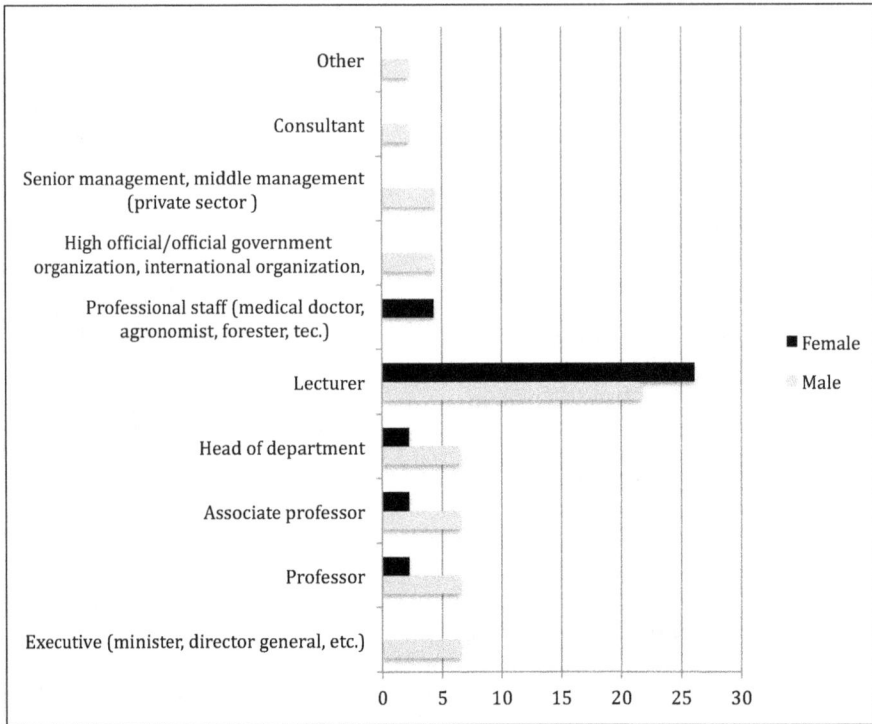

a few graduates had reached high positions within the university and in other sectors of society, but many remained in the position they had held before entering the PhD training program. Many respondents brought up the fact that the training had not led to career advancement in terms of higher positions. However, this had little to do with thwarted ambitions. Instead, continuance in the position of lecturer turned out to be a deliberate choice made on the basis of more time for research. Many respondent lecturers asserted that the PhD degree had served an important function by increasing their status as researchers, and given the limited time and resources available for research, a lectureship was the closest to research. The positions of rector, vice dean, dean or head of department were viewed as administrative and as stepping away from the role of researcher.

> Being a lecturer is more in line with my ambition as a researcher. You know, we have very little resources for research and time is limited, but having that position allows for at least some space to do research. I look at my colleagues being deans and head of department, they are all absorbed with other duties. (man)

> I saw a good opportunity to develop when I was offered the position as vice dean, but I see it as the temporary position it is. So far, I have not been able to do any research, which is sad. The administration has been heavy and the salary

is only marginally higher, so when my period is over I think I will go back to my previous position as lecturer. (man)

A striking feature is the relatively low proportion of women in higher positions in academia. Women make up only one-third of professorships, heads of department or associate professorships. This will be further elaborated below.

The university's working conditions was generally described as poor, both in terms of access to infrastructure such as computers, laboratories and other equipment and in terms of salaries. Most respondents stated it was difficult to live on a university salary, not to mention support a whole family. From the survey and interviews it became clear other sources of income were needed. Reportedly, the main source of supplementary income was consultancy work in combination with teaching at private universities. In the survey, almost 68 per cent stated they were involved in more than one income-generating activity.

If I didn't do consultancy my private life would be very difficult, yes, very difficult. You cannot survive on the salaries paid here at the university. (man)

You know when you do consultancy; it can be your salary for a whole year [...] yes, I need that, because our working conditions at university are not good. For example, when I'm lecturing I use my own transportation, sometimes we say that we have to pay for work. In terms of that I'm not happy, the working conditions are very tough, the computers are always broken and this is a research institution, we need computers. (woman)

The need for supplementary income was evident in all academic fields and across gender. Another dominant theme was that consultancy work is in varying degree integrated into the infrastructure of universities. This means that individual researchers as well as university departments can be the main recipients of these assignments. Differences emerged between academic fields as regards the ease or difficulty of finding extra income. Applied disciplines, such as veterinary sciences, were generally considered to be better placed in this respect than disciplines such as fine arts.

There was also a difference in general view of consultancy. While some respondents perceived consultancy as acceptable but not desirable, others were actually keen to have a balance between academic and consultancy work. In this respect, researchers particularly stressed the possibility of applying their research to other sectors of society and of spreading their competence. Sometimes, students were involved in consultancies, through which they got funding or empirical material for their Master's essays. Thus, consultancy work became a way of contributing to capacity building.

I wanted to do something that translates science into practical work. It is a motivation for me because I wanted to see that my research is used. The university

also encourages staff to go to the applied sector; we not only want to be theoretical [...] I think it is very good and important because we need to show our
graduates that they should look at their future, to find work in society, and they
need to look at science not as something isolated from society but to see to the
applied side of science. (man)

A majority of respondents stressed that their PhD training has had a great impact on their lives, both professionally and personally. Even those who had not
climbed the career ladder still felt their status in society had changed and that
they could interact in intellectual settings with greater confidence. Many also
emphasised the strategic position of PhD graduates in the development of the
country. Even though the impact of training on respondents' lives had reportedly been high, follow-up questions about its importance for current work position
and of the importance of having a PhD degree revealed a somewhat different
picture. Since many graduates had returned to their previous positions as lecturers, the impact of PhD training on advancement was low. In these instances,
the impact was shown to be more related to higher status. When looking at
respondents' perceptions of correspondence between work tasks and qualifications, almost 21 per cent reported that their current work tasks corresponded
only to a small extent with their academic qualifications. Within this group, all
reported feeling over-qualified. No variation was found when controlling for
gender or discipline. The feeling of over-qualification was strongly linked to the
relative absence of research in the work tasks:

I perform much of the same things today as I did before going for my PhD
studies. I see my training as something that was aimed to qualify me for doing
research. Now with this increasing teaching load and no resources for research
I feel a bit over-qualified. It is quite frustrating, like having a driving licence but
not being allowed to drive. (man)

A significant difference was found between men and women with regard to degree of independence. Men seem to experience more dissatisfaction than women
regarding the degree of independence associated with their positions. To a lesser
degree, women showed more dissatisfaction in relation to contribution to society and opportunities for career development. Notably, the latter is linked
with the gender distribution of positions at the university, which display under-
representation of women in higher positions (see polar 7.8).

Controlling for academic discipline revealed no major variation. Medicine
stands out to some extent on degree of independence and intellectual challenge.
Respondents from the social sciences and humanities reported somewhat higher
dissatisfaction in relation to opportunities for career development and social
status.

Polar 7.8 Percentage of graduates dissatisfied with their position by gender and reason for dissatisfaction

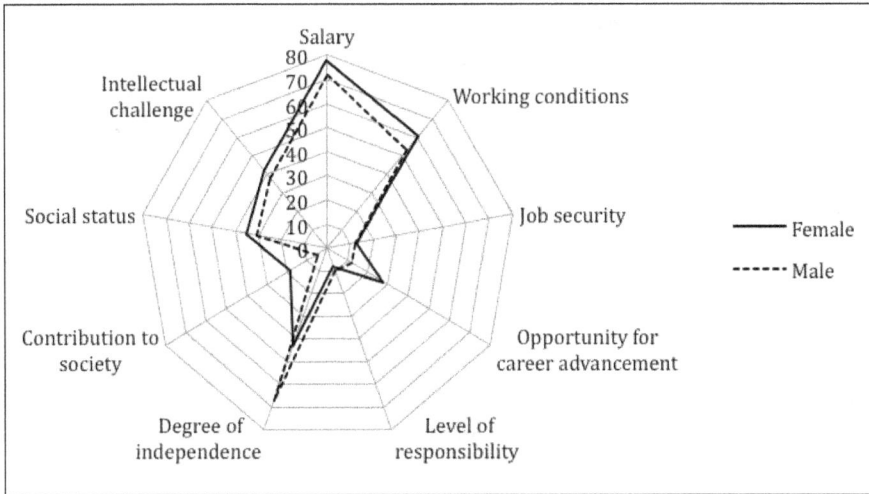

Polar 7.9 Percentage of graduates experiencing discrimination in current work position by gender and reason for discrimination

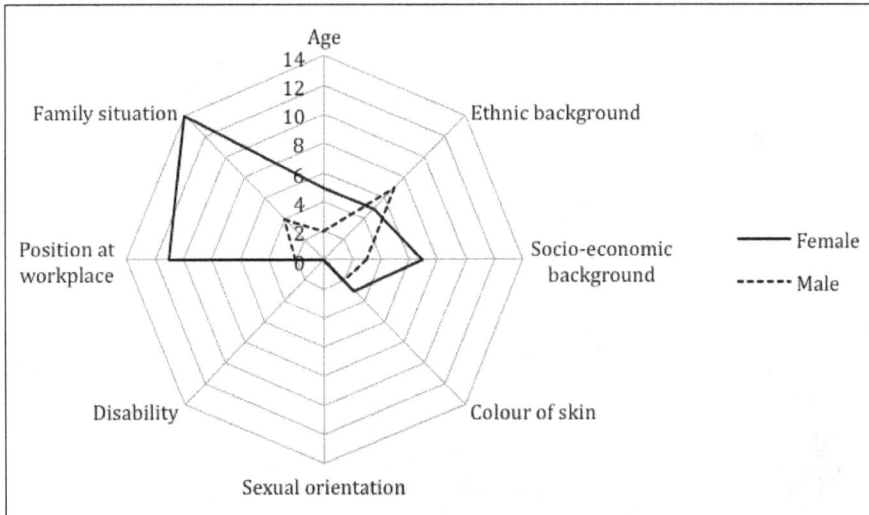

Following on the question of experience of discrimination during training, the same question was asked about their current positions. This time, the question only concerned the current workplace, not the interactions with society at large. As displayed in Polar 7.9, female respondents reported a relatively higher incidence of discrimination on the basis of position at the workplace and family situation. Women also scored proportionally higher on the variables of age and socioeconomic background as reasons for discrimination. No significant variations were found across academic disciplines.

The survey results indicate that women to emphasised these experiences to a greater extent than men. In other words, women's experience of these problems was stronger. We cannot know if women have been more frequently exposed to such problems than men, as this would require a different type of data. However, we do have information on the subjective experience of researchers. These are interesting to explore since they contain information on how women and men talk about the micro-politics of the academy (Morley 1999). Micro-politics reveal how everyday work relations are, among other things, gendered. This information is important since it uncovers how gender differences in academic careers are, in a longer perspective, produced and maintained (Singer *et al.*1999).

The interviews indicated that researchers had different opinions on the role and impact of gender relations on the academy and on academic careers in particular. When asked directly in interviews, few researchers said they had experienced discrimination based on gender or any other grounds, such as ethnicity, race or social class.

Instead, experiences of discrimination or other negative treatment were revealed in more subtle ways. In varying degree, the interviewed researchers perceived that it was easier for men than women to pursue an academic career in Mozambique, but men were slightly more positive about women's career possibilities. Perhaps more interesting to analyse are the explanations given for the poor representation of women researchers at the university. The explanations given are here categorised into two main themes for analytical reasons. These themes to a varying degree emphasises "external" (factors outside university such as family situation or social class) vs. "internal" factors such as workplace relations. From gender research on labour relations we know that the division between private and public is mainly possible at a theoretical level, as these relations are often intermingled in practice (Hartman 1986). In the context of this research the division between the private and the public represents a dominant strand in the attribution of responsibility. The following quotation gives words to this.

> Here at the university we don't discriminate. No, women and men have the same opportunities. No the reason is outside, because of women's bigger responsibilities outside universities, women have a more difficult finding time and support for pursing an academic career. (man)

This category of explanation emphasises structures outside the university, such as family situation or social class, as the main explanation for the lower representation of women researchers in universities. This explanation is widely accepted and referred to by both women and men. In this context, one woman suggested that her lack of family obligations was a main factor in her success in academia. Another woman suggested that her privileged family situation, both in terms of socioeconomic status and support from her extended family, had been crucial in the development of her academic career.

> Yes, I come from a privileged background, yes that helped a lot and my mother in-law, she took care of my children while I was away. Yes, that has been very important for my career. (woman)

The second explanatory category offers a mixture of explanations, which include both internal (such as gender relations at work) and external factors (gender relations outside university work).

> – Of course it is easier for men to pursue and academic career!
> – Why?
> – Because, men get a lot of support [...] I know men who have got financial support from the university to complete their PhD after their training period was finished, something that I didn't get [...] men are always going around, getting the information, yes, about calls, when women get information it is always too late and the deadline is close. And some of us don't have access to internet. We don't have computers.[...] and sometimes women are not supported by their partners and they have small children, yes, because of that they refrain. (woman)

The division between private and public in the first quotation is expressed in terms of placing responsibility on structures outside the university and on women. By contrast, the second explanation opens up a variety of factors for analysis, such as the gendered nature of university organisation in general and university work relations in particular, as well as the non-functioning of meritocratic principles in universities. As such, it places responsibility on how men act and highlights the need for structural analysis.

An intersectional analysis of these quotations suggests that gender, age, family situation and socioeconomic background mutually constitute differing conditions for career advancement. This analysis supports the statistical analysis of experiences of discrimination where women experienced more discrimination along family situation, socio economic background and at the workplace. More research is needed to understand the full implications of this.

7.2.2 Research output and collaboration

The great majority of surveyed graduates with positions in academia had continued to do research in varying measure and all respondents expressed a strong desire to continue doing research. However, the survey results indicate some variation between women and men and between disciplines in terms of allocation time on research. As shown in Diagram 7.3, close to 90 per cent of respondents with positions in academia spend 25 per cent or less of full-time on research.

Diagram 7.3 Percentage of time spent on research by gender

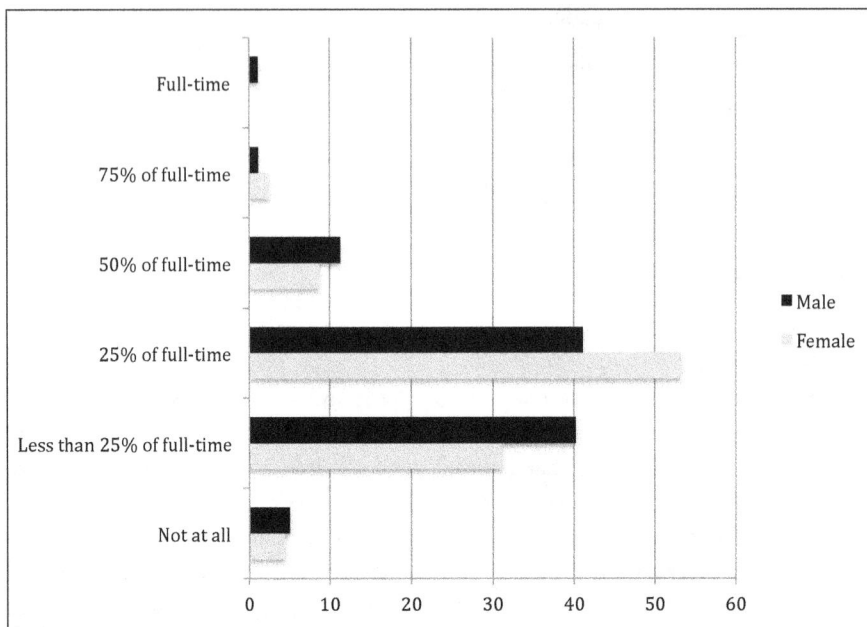

Women represent the larger share of those spending 25 per cent of full-time on research, and men in the category spending less than 25 per cent of full-time. In total, men are better represented in the categories 50 per cent of full-time up to full-time.

Looking at the distribution of time spent on research in different academic disciplines, the results show significant variation. As displayed in Diagram 7.4, in total graduates in agricultural science and science seem to spend the largest share of full-time on research, followed by technology and medicine. Interestingly, there is comparatively low research activity in the social sciences and humanities. Close to all respondents in these fields reported research activity of 25 per cent or less.

Generally, the amount of time that can be spent on research varies according to both available time and resources, both being reportedly scarce at UEM. In particular, lack of research funding appeared to be a difficult issue. In response to questions about their source of funding, quite a few respondents reported that they conducted research without support from the university, government or any other external provider.[42] Among those reporting external support for research, 56.3 per cent of the funds came from international donors, followed by international research foundations (23.7 per cent) and the government (20.0

---

42. This question was posed only in the interviews, not in the survey. That is why it is not statistically reported.

Diagram 7.4 Percentage of time spent on research by academic discipline

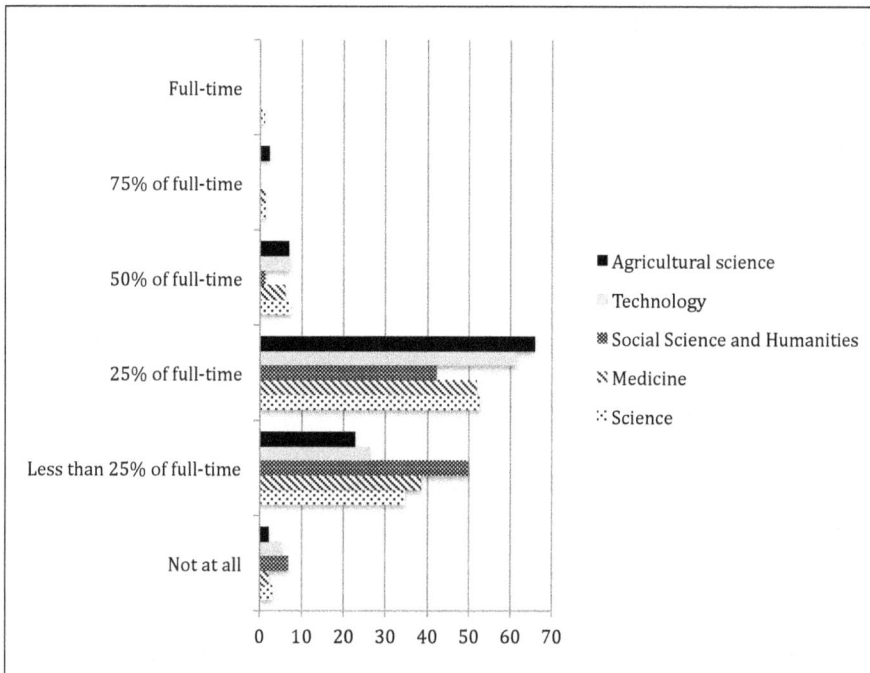

per cent). The disciplines reporting the largest external funds were the STEM sciences, with science at the top. Social sciences and the humanities benefited significantly less from external research funding.

An important factor for the quality of research output is access to and participation in different forms of research collaboration and networks. While some respondents maintained contact with their previous research department in Sweden and South Africa, most new research collaborations and networks evolved after PhD graduation and are with researchers in countries in the region.

> I coordinate a sub-Saharan network and the universities involved are located in South Africa, Botswana, Tanzania and Zimbabwe. I'm the country representative in the network. The network is about information and disseminating knowledge in our knowledge area. (man, engineering)

The degree of participation in research networks was reportedly high among respondents. Survey results show that more than 52 per cent were involved in some type of international research network, 48 per cent in some Pan-African or regional research network and 72 per cent in some national research network. Science and medicine stood out as the disciplines reporting the highest participation in all network categories. The lowest participation was among respondents in the social sciences, humanities and in technology. No significant variation when controlling for gender was found.

Diagram 7.5 Percentage of graduates reporting research collaboration by region and type of collaboration

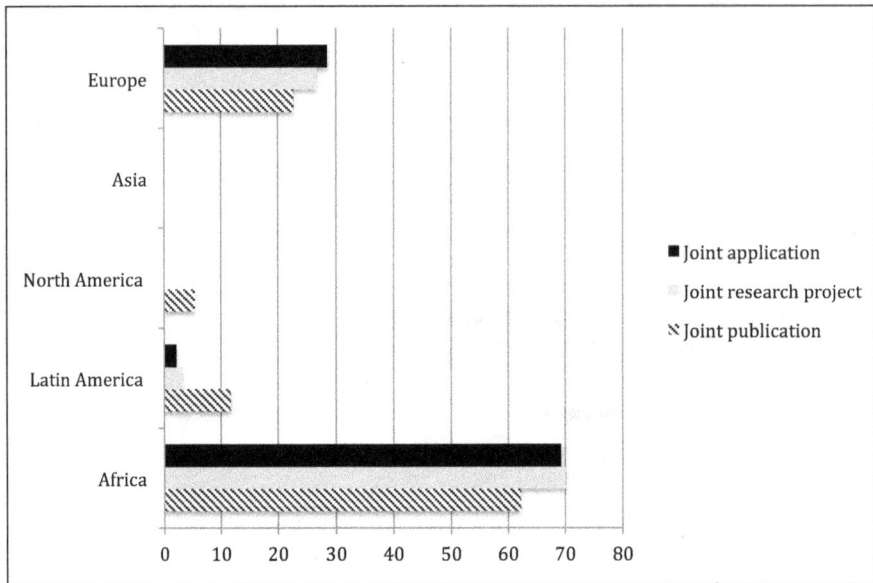

Diagram 7.6 Percentage of graduates reporting publication by academic discipline and type of publication

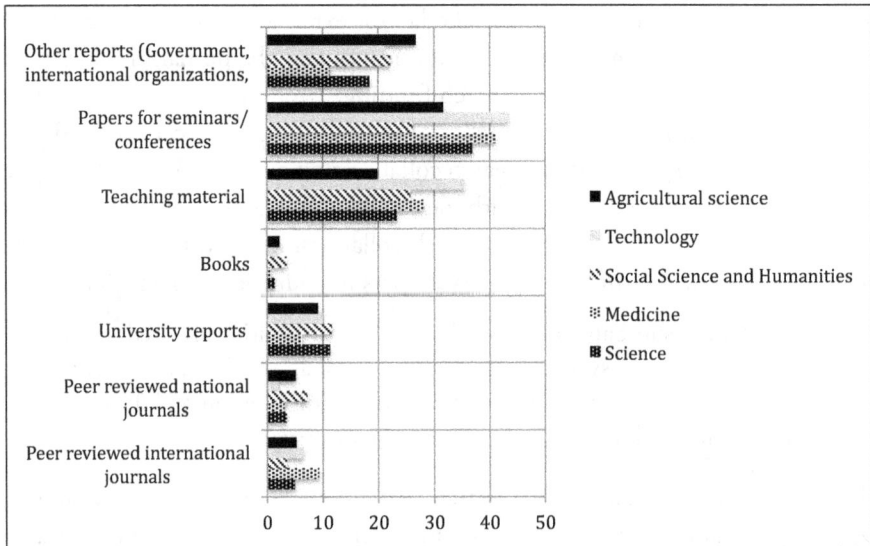

The degree of contact and collaboration with the former training institution in Sweden or South Africa was relatively high. More than 73 per cent reported some form of contact. The dominant form was research collaboration (66.7 per cent) followed by supervision (16.7 per cent) and lecturing (12.6 per cent). The proportion of types of contact was quite evenly distributed among the disciplines. Close to 47 per cent of responding graduates with positions in academia reported some form of research collaboration with partners outside Mozambique. Looking at the extent of research collaboration in relation to region and type of collaboration, the results displayed in Diagram 7.5 show that collaboration with African researchers and institutions represents the greater share of the three types of collaboration itemised in the diagram. Europe made up the larger share of collaborations outside Africa. Notably, no collaborations of any type existed with Asian partners.

The relative lack of collaboration outside Africa was explained in terms of the difficulty of getting funding and complicated bidding procedures. A male engineering researcher noted:

> If I want to collaborate with somebody in Mozambique or in the region, it is at a personal level, I just do it. It is very easy with e-mail: if the collaboration involves researchers from Sweden or other regions, it must pass through the university or the government, and then it becomes complicated. (man)

The sampled graduates' research output varied in terms of type of publication. Taken together, papers for seminars and conferences, teaching materials, reports to government agencies and to some extent university reports constituted the larger part of published output. Peer-reviewed books and articles in national and international journals were reportedly produced to a significant lesser extent. As displayed in Diagram 7.6, the types of publication varied to some extent between disciplines. A significantly larger share of reports to government and international organisations was evident among agricultural science graduates as compared to medicine. One the other hand, medicine has the largest representation of all disciplines in peer-reviewed international journals. Graduates in social science and humanities have a significant lower share of seminar and conference papers compared to other disciplines, but the highest share of university reports.

7.2.3 Geographical and sectoral mobility

The degree of mobility among responding graduates was in general low with regard to sectoral, vertical and geographical mobility. The great majority (76.1 per cent) reported having less than three positions since graduation. Less than 18 per cent reported having three or four positions and 11 per cent reported five to six positions. As shown in Diagram 7.7, mobility in terms of number of positions since graduation seems to be greater among men. The representation of women in the upper categories is significantly lower. The results indicate no significant variation when controlling for discipline.[43]

---

43. For obvious reasons, there is a comparison bias in the result base: since no distinction has been made on the basis of year of graduation, the results apply equally to new graduates and to graduates from, say, the early 1990s.

Diagram 7.7 Percentages of graduates by number of positions and gender

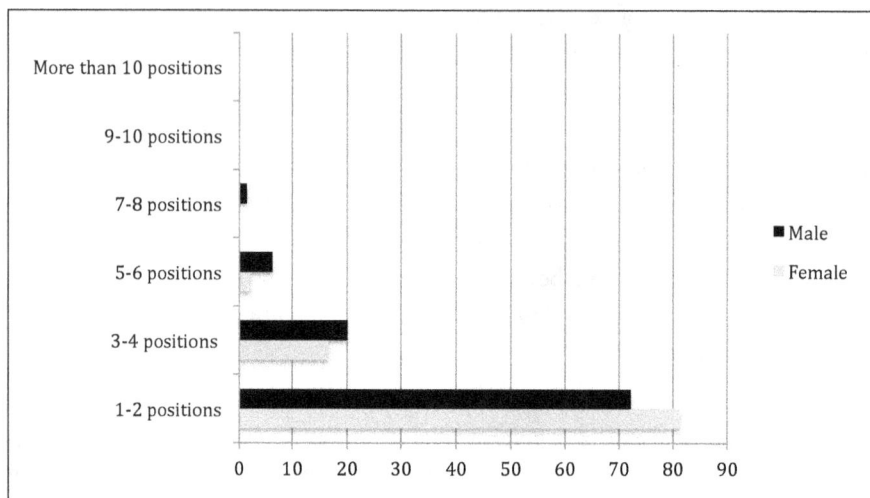

As has been shown, sectoral mobility among surveyed graduates was quite low. The great majority have remained at the university since graduation. A few have tried other employment outside the university, but many of them seem to have returned. When asking this category of respondents about employment outside the university since graduation, 53.6 per cent reported working in other government sectors, preferably positions in ministries. A significant share had also worked in the private sector (16.2 per cent) and for international donors (11.8 per cent). Another 10.2 per cent had also been self-employed, with a business of their own, preferably as consultants. As the above diagram reveals, sectoral mobility among women was significantly lower than for men.

A notable theme in the interviews was the strong desire to remain in academia, despite poor working conditions. The theme of giving back, appreciating what they had once been given and contributing to capacity building was repeatedly brought up and acknowledged by many respondents. The quote below reveals feelings of loyalty towards the body that had had a clear impact on the informant's career choice.

> I would have preferred to stay 100 per cent at the university but with my involvement in state politics it was not possible. University teaching is my only way of staying in contact with an academic career and I think I have something valuable to give to the students [...] But it is hard, you feel like you give and give and sometimes you feel exhausted [...] In Mozambique, unfortunately, if you are educated there are so many gaps to fill, where I am now at the ministry I have to do my own job at the same time as I train others. (woman)

In the quotation above it is also clear how feelings of loyalty had actually prevented the person from pursuing an academic career. The quote also underscores the strategically important positions PhD holders have at the university as well as in other sectors of society. While these descriptions were accompanied by feelings of pride and satisfaction, they also revealed the tremendous workload and perceived onus of responsibility on respondents, and the associated feelings of exhaustion and frustration.

Given low levels of sectoral and vertical mobility among graduates, geographical mobility was low as well. Of the responding graduates, only 16.8 per cent reported working abroad after graduation. Of these, 41 per cent were women and 59 per cent were men. Respondents in medicine, science and agricultural science had a slightly higher representation compared to other disciplines. Social science and the humanities displayed the lowest levels of geographical mobility. An interesting observation, though not a surprising one, was the relatively high representation of younger graduates among those with experience of working abroad. Compared with graduates from the 1990s, there is slightly greater geographical mobility among those graduating after 2000.

To better understand the incentives for geographical mobility, respondents were asked to rate a number of aspects believed to be of importance in deciding to work abroad. The result shows that working conditions, salary and career-development opportunities were rated as very important aspects. Surprisingly, development opportunities for family members as well as language/culture were largely rated as being unimportant or of minor importance.

8. Conclusions and policy implications

In this final chapter, conclusions will be drawn from the results presented within the two main themes of the study: I) organisation of and experience during the period of PhD training and II) career development after graduation: positions, working conditions and mobility. A set of policy recommendations will be made for each theme.

8.1 Theme I: Organisation of and experience during the period of PhD training

Overall, support for research capacity-building in Mozambique seems to have been organised much in accordance with Sida's established principles for research support, that is, a focus on one principal research institution and support for PhD training as a core activity. During the period under investigation, the sandwich model was operationalised as the sole modality for training, and mainly targeted candidates holding staff positions at UEM. In this period, the role of Swedish universities as counterpart institutions for implementing the program has gradually been supplemented by growing collaboration with South African universities.

The process of recruitment to the PhD training program was not within the scope of this study, but from the survey results it can be concluded that admission to the program has been largely confined to one group, UEM staff members. The continued focus on staff members as the only eligible group for admission to the training program gives rise to concerns about the extent to which candidates are selected on a competitive basis and the quality implications of such strategy. This is so since suitability for research training does not always correlate with position.

As a result of the policy of targeting staff members, candidates start their training relatively late in life. Even though the adopted data-collection method precludes exact calculation of average age, the results indicate that most respondents started their training somewhere between 35 and 40. This is considerably higher than the age of PhD candidates in Sweden, where since 1990 the average commencement age has been 29 (HSV 2012). An interesting conclusion requiring further consideration is the tendency towards later starts among female candidates than men. Childbearing and greater family responsibilities are the principal impediments to earlier commencement by women. Age of commencement is an important factor in the long-term outcome of the investments in PhD training, since number of years as active researcher have a direct bearing on the extent of the contribution to local research capacity-building: for obvious reasons, a person graduating at 35 will have more time to contribute to research capacity-building than someone graduating at 50, with 10 or 15 years left to retirement.

Dissertation by articles has gradually become the dominant form of dissertation across all disciplines. This form seems to largely match the mobile premises of the sandwich model, allowing for clear checkpoints along the way.

Insufficient local resources for research and co-supervision at UEM seem to be the most problematic areas in the training situation, regardless of gender, discipline or country of training (Sweden and South Africa). The lack of improvements observed over time (1990–2012) in these areas gives rise to concerns about the long-term effectiveness of the program's capacity-building potential, since research resources and co-supervision are fundamental to building and sustaining local PhD programs and research. Lack of involvement by and time among co-supervisors and inadequate funding for research infrastructure, particularly in STEM sciences seem to be the principal underlying factor for the dissatisfaction. A notable observation was the somewhat higher representation of female graduates and candidates reporting dissatisfaction with co-supervision. A higher degree of dissatisfaction with Swedish supervision was observed among candidates compared to graduates, again with an over-representation of female respondents. Further research is required into the underlying explanations for this: whether dissatisfaction derives from changes among the candidates or in the organisation and performance of supervision in Sweden. However, generally the results support international research findings, since it is well known that female PhD students are more likely to be exposed to negative treatment and subtle discrimination in informal everyday situations, PhD supervision sessions being frequently mentioned as an example (Fox and Long 1991, Caplan 1994, Mählck 2001).

One of the more notable conclusions to be drawn from the results on the experience of training is the significantly higher level of dissatisfaction among graduates and candidates that have done or were doing their training at South African universities, compared to their Swedish equivalents. Access to supervisors and quality of supervision is the dominant practical problem facing PhD students. The level of dissatisfaction with supervision is relatively constant over time, indicating deficiencies in communication between PhD students, home institution and host institution, and/or unwillingness on the South African and Mozambican side to make improvements. Hence, further research is required into the training conditions among this group of students.

The international profile of the host institution in terms of the number of international students and staff seems to be important for having experienced the host department positively. The presence of other temporary-stay international students and researchers makes it easier to connect and share problems – in this case adapting practically and socially to the situation in the host department and society at large. In addition, an international presence is also important for the academic outcome of training, since it contributes to a more vibrant and multidimensional research discussion.

The sources of dissatisfaction with the training situation did not vary across academic discipline, but the dissatisfaction with resources was more clearly expressed among graduates and candidates in the sciences and medicine. Not surprisingly, these disciplines suffer most from the absence of research facilities such as laboratories and technical equipment.

The times spent at the host institution were the most productive periods for the candidates during their training. Two primary factors are of relevance in this regard: the absence of disruptive activities (teaching, administration, caring responsibilities and family life) and the experience of loneliness and isolation. The two latter factors are worrisome indications of the price paid by candidates to obtain a PhD.

In general, there is a positive attitude to the idea and premises of the sandwich model, but findings also indicate that the mobile character of the modality has different effects on women and men. To a much greater extent, men stay for longer periods in country of training, both in total and on average, than women. Family responsibilities seem to be the main factor preventing women from staying longer. The inability to spend sufficient time in the country of training, which reportedly is necessary to fully concentrate on research, placed women under greater pressure. In addition, shorter stays by women could result in looser and more insecure relations with the host department and supervisor in particular, which may in part explain the higher dissatisfaction with the training situation reported by women.

The study paid particular attention to the presence of discrimination in the training situation experienced by graduates and candidates, both at UEM and in the country of training. From the results, it can be concluded that the main discriminatory expressions at work at UEM were on the basis of family situation and position at the workplace. Women experience discrimination in these areas significantly more than men. The survey indicated similar patterns of discrimination experiences based on skin -colour while in the country of training in (i.e South Africa and Sweden). However these experiences were differently articulated in the interviews.

Policy implications

As displayed, the Mozambican higher education and research system still hosts comparatively few individuals holding PhD degrees. This, along with persisting weak research structures in most higher learning institutions and the current massification of undergraduate programs, constitutes a strong argument for continuing to concentrate resources on UEM, where the preconditions for building research capacity are most favourable.

Suitability for research training does not necessarily correspond with seniority and position. The recruitment process is an important and sensitive area for further policy work and research, because the individual characteristics of candidates in terms of age, gender, qualifications and not least suitability all have implications for career development and mobility. Future policy work should consider options for more competitive recruitment processes through, for example, open calls, which will enable the intake of qualified and suitable candidates, including from postgraduate programs.

The situation of female candidates in the program needs to be acknowledged. Special attention should be given to the problem of entry into the program at a later age faced by female applicants – perhaps by allowing for a later start by female candidates. Also germane are the too short stays in country of training due to family responsibilities, resulting in deficiencies of supervision and lack of time for research.

The situation of co-supervision at UEM needs to be acknowledged. The program should initiate discussion among stakeholders on how to improve conditions for co-supervision. This is crucial, since an active and deliberate policy on co-supervision is indispensable to the emergence of local PhD programs at UEM.

In addition, different types of discrimination in the training situation, both at UEM and in the country of training, need to be tackled by stakeholders. Of particular importance is the situation of candidates training in South African institutions.

8.2 Theme II: Mobility and career development after graduation: positions and working conditions

Regardless of gender and academic discipline, a significant share of researchers trained in the program during the period 1990-2012 have remained at UEM. Despite reportedly low salaries and increasing workloads, UEM is still the most attractive workplace for most graduates. The fact that all held staff positions at the time of recruitment to the PhD program may serve as one explanation. Among graduates reporting having left UEM, mainly for positions in government agencies or other universities in the country, a considerable number retained some connection to UEM, mostly teaching. Taken together, the goal set for the program – training individuals to establish research capacity at UEM – seems to have been met, at least in term of the individuals in place at UEM.

The relatively low number of staff members holding PhD degrees at UEM has meant fast career development for some of the graduates, both in their departments and in the university administration. Notably, women represent a significantly lower share of those who have achieved a high position at UEM. This confirms the results from earlier studies of women's career development in academia, which indicate a significantly higher presence of women in lower positions.

Supplementary income from consultancies is widespread among graduates and is an accepted part of academic life at UEM. A noteworthy conclusion from the interviews is that, in the context of weak research resources at UEM, consultancy does not necessarily draw attention away from research but may also be a channel for applying and communicating already produced research results. Consultancy could also enable the identification of new research areas and questions and capacity building. Researchers often conducted research as part of their consultancy work. This was particularly evident in the sciences and engineering.

Even though the attainment of a PhD has meant a lot to many of the graduates, the degree has been more important in boosting their status and self-confidence than for the actual work. The correspondence between the intended application of the PhD degree and the actual work at UEM was low for a considerable share of the graduates, leaving a feeling of being over-qualified among many of them. Basically, many performed the same duties after graduation as they had before entering the training program. Lack of resources to conduct research stands out as the principal factor impeding the application and transmission of the acquired academic skills.

Salary, working conditions and degree of independence stand out as the principal sources of dissatisfaction among the graduates. The results are mainly applicable to graduates with positions at UEM. Apart from dissatisfaction with salaries, which is comparably absolute in character, the other two factors (which are intimately linked) involve more complex sets of explanatory factors requiring more in-depth analysis. An initial hypothesis in such analysis is that the increasing teaching load and administrative burden experienced by many graduates constitute the main variables. These factors, along with the somewhat higher dissatisfaction with career-advancement opportunities experienced by female graduates, need also to be further studied in relation to structures and expressions of different types of power.

Intimately linked to working conditions is the potential presence and expression of different forms of discrimination in the workplace. From the survey results, it can be concluded that female graduates seem to experience more discrimination in their current work positions than males. Still, the survey results indicate lower levels of discrimination experienced among the graduates, which was also confirmed by the results of the interviews. Unlike the candidates, the interviewed graduates were generally unwilling to talk about their experience of discrimination. Paraphrasing Paul Willis's theory of personal trouble and public problems, it has been suggested that reluctance to talk about problems in academia is built on a general fear of "becoming the problem," which in a longer perspective also reinforces the tendency to individualise problems of discrimination in the academy (Mählck 2003). However, as gender research has shown, the reluctance to talk about experiences of discrimination in academia doesn't mean that discriminating practices don't exist (Morley 1999,Mählck 2003, Bennet 2002, Mabukela & Magubane 2004). From studies in Commonwealth universities, we know that women are systematically excluded from processes of recruitment and from social and informal networks. Women have less access to university infrastructure and career possibilities and are more sexually harassed and/or belittled at universities compared to men (Morley *et al.* 2003, 2006). So far, there is little comparative research on how structures of inequality in the academy are produced and maintained. In this growing field, there are indications that similar, although not identical, processes of inclusion/exclusion based on gender and race are at work in academic workplaces in different geopolitical places (Morley 2006, Thaver and Mählck 2010). Against this backdrop of an apparently global pattern of gendered inequality and gender-based discrimination in higher education institutions, we suggest that the findings from this study constitute no exception, although more research is needed into how and why these mechanisms are produced and maintained as well as into forms of resistance.

The willingness to conduct research is much greater than the resources and time available. The great majority of graduates have continued to do research, but on a quite small scale. Less the 10 per cent of the graduates spend 50 per cent or more of their time on research, regardless of gender. Graduates in the social sciences and humanities, being the disciplines requiring fewest resources for research, reported the lowest research activity. This finding has not been investigated further in this study, but an explanation could be the greater expansion of undergraduate students in these disciplines and the increased teaching load flowing from that. Regardless of the variations among disciplines, the conclusion on the volume of research activities among the graduates is on the whole quite discouraging. Generally, long-term support to raise research qualifications among staff members at UEM has not resulted in a noteworthy expansion and intensification of research activity. This is further confirmed by the reported feeling of doing the same work after entering PhD training as before. Lack of resources for research after graduation, along with increasing demand for undergraduate teaching are the two main impediments to the emergence of a research culture at UEM. Consequently, research capacity-building at UEM does not keep pace with the current expansion of undergraduate enrolment. This situation will persist for as long as the main political priority for UEM is as provider of tertiary education and not research.

In contrast to the intense policy and academic discussion of the problem of brain drain among highly skilled individuals originating in African countries, the conclusion from this study suggests remarkably low mobility among the PhD graduates, geographical as well as sectoral. Since graduation, the great majority of the graduates have remained in Mozambique and as staff members at UEM. Accordingly, the support for PhD training has definitely resulted in the building of a foundation for research at UEM in terms of qualified individuals. While a low degree of mobility means a higher availability of qualified individuals at UEM, it could also mean loss of the competencies, experience and contacts acquired through mobility. In this regard, it has been suggested that the mobility of researchers is an indicator of their competence and flexibility (MORE 2010). Lack of attractive offers for career development abroad or in other sectors of Mozambican society and feelings of loyalty towards UEM were given as explanations for the relative absence of mobility. Another explanation could be that the low research activity per se has hampered participation in international research programs and networks, which in turn has resulted in less exposure to positions abroad and incentives to look for them. In any event, the factors underlying the low mobility, as well as the conditions for mobility among this group need to be further studied.

Policy implications

The conditions for research at UEM need to be strengthened. Measures are needed to counter the current low pay-off for having a PhD degree in terms of ability to conduct research. If UEM is to be a centre of excellence in both the country's tertiary education system and in scientific production, current resources going to undergraduate training must be supplemented by additional resources for research. One possible way forward is to construct different postdoctoral programs, for research at UEM and abroad. To raise UEM's international research profile, there is also a need to consider developing sabbatical programs that will encourage leading international researchers to spend their sabbaticals in Mozambican institutions, thus allowing high-quality interaction between local researchers and their international colleagues.

The conditions for career development among female graduates needs be acknowledged. This study indicates difficulties for women in reaching higher university positions, and there is a need to initiate discussion of the factors underlying this situation. Explanations emphasise structural issues, the researchers' individual dispositions and the relationship between researchers and institutions, but they also need to highlight the responsibility of higher education institutions and their key representatives, such as donors, rectors, heads of department and program coordinators, rather than placing all the responsibility on individual women or families. This is not to suggest that gender differences in the private sphere do not cause problems for women academics. On the contrary, it is important to take all the aspects of women's lives into account in building a research landscape that is open to research talents regardless of gender or the other social relations that currently produce differing conditions for research.

There is reason for concern regarding the low mobility shown among the graduates. In the global competition between universities, degree of internationalisation has become crucial element in success and positioning. A high degree of mobility among students and researchers is perhaps the most important factor for successful internationalisation, since a high inflow and outflow of researchers and students is assumed to increase the quality of the institution's activities. To prevent UEM from becoming isolated from the international sphere of higher education and research, there is a need to acknowledge the problem of low mobility, particularly among researchers. Construction of different postdoctoral and sabbatical programs could be a way to increase mobility and, ultimately, the quality of research activities at UEM.

References

African Development Bank. 2012. Briefing Note 5: Income inequality in Africa. Briefing notes for AfDB's long-term strategy.

Allwood, C.M. 2004. Perspektiv på den kvalitativa idétraditionen. In C.M. Allwood (ed.), *Perspektiv på kvalitativ metod*. Lund Student Litteratur, pp. 9–35.

Anyanwu, J.C. 2012. Developing knowledge for economic advancement in Africa. *International journal of academic research in economics and management sciences*, Vol. 1, No. 2.

Altbach, P. 2013. The global brain race – Robbing developing countries. *University World News Global Edition*, Issue 268.

Auriol, L., M. Schaaper and B. Felix. 2012. Mapping Careers and Mobility of Doctorate Holders: Draft Guidelines, Model Questionnaire and Indicators – Third Edition. OECD Science, Technology and Industry Working Papers, 2012/07. OECD, Paris.

Auriol, L. 2010. Careers of doctorate holders: Employment and mobility patterns. STI Working Paper 2010/4. Statistical analysis of science, technology and industry. OECD, Paris.

Beintema, N.M, P. Pardey and J. Roseboom. 1998. Educating agricultural researchers: A review of the role of African universities. EPTD Discussion Paper No, 36. Washington DC.

Bennet J, 2002. Exploring a "Gap": Strategisising Gender Equity in African Universites. Feminist Africa Intellectual politics. Issue 1 2002 pp 34–64.

Bloom. D, D. Canning and K. Chan. 2005. *Higher education and economic development in Africa*. Harvard UP, Cambridge MA.

Empririca GmbH. 2005. Post-docs in the Life Sciences. Paper prepared for the NetReAct project.

Chapman, D. and A. Austin. 2002. *The changing context of higher education in the developing world*. Greenwood Press, Place[?].

Caplan, P. 1994. Lifting a ton of feathers. A womans guide for surviving in the academic world. University of Toronto Press.

Chilundo, A. 2002. The state of higher education in Mozambique. Paper presented at UNESCO African regional conference, Progress and future directions in Africa. Abuja, Nigeria.

Cole, J. and B. Singer. 1991. A theory of limited differences. Explaining the productivity puzzle in science. In H. Zuckerman, *J. Cole* and J. Bruer (eds), *The Outer Circle: Women in the Scientific Community*. Norton, New York.

Commission of the European Communities. 2008. Better careers and more mobility: A European partnership for research. Communication from Commission to the Council and the European Parliament, PLACE[?].

Connell, R. 2007. *Southern theory: The global dynamics of knowledge in social science*. Cambridge, Polity Press.

Currie, J., P. Harris and B.Thiele. 2000. Sacrifices in greedy universities: Are they gendered? *Gender and Education,* Vol. 12, No. 3, pp.269–91.

Docquier, F. and A. Marfouk. 2006. International migration by educational attainment. In C. Ozden and M. Schiff (eds), *International migration, remittances and development?* Palgrave MacMillan, New York.

European Union. 2012. A European research area partnership for excellence and growth. Publication Office of the European Union, Luxembourg

European Union. 2012. The state of the innovation union 2012: Accelerating change. Directorate-General for Research and Innovation. European Commission, Publication Office of the European Union, Luxembourg.

European Union. 2010. Europe 2020: A strategy for smart, sustainable and inclusive growth. Communication from the Commission, Brussels.

Global University Network for Innovation (GUNI). 2008. Higher education in the world: New challenges and emerging roles for human and social development. Palgrave MacMillan, PLACE[?].

Institute for Prospective Technology Studies and European Commission. 2007. Intra-EU mobility of researchers. PLACE [?].

International Monetary Fund. 2013. World Economic Outlook Update 2013. International Monetary Fund, Washington DC.

Harding, S. 2009. Postcolonial and feminist philosophies of science and technology: convergences and dissonances. *Postcolonial Studies*, Vol. 12, Issue 4, pp.401–21.

Hoba, P. and A. Marfouk. 2011. Why should we worry about brain drain from Africa? *Journal of the European higher education area.* Issue 4.

Högskoleverkets (HSV). 2012. Högskoleverkets årsrapport 2012. .

Husu, L. 2001. *Sexism, Support and Survival in Academia. Academic Women and Hidden Discrimination in Finland.* University of Helsinki, Social Psychological Studies 6, Raabe Academic Publishers, Berlin.

Hoffman, D. 2009. Changing academic mobility patterns and international migration. What will academic mobility mean in the 21st century. *Journal of Studies in International Education*, Vol. 13, No. 3, pp. 347–64.

Jerven, M. 2013. Poor numbers: how we are misled by African development statistics and what to do about it. Cornell Studies in Political Economy.

Jöns, H. 2010 Transnational academic mobility and

Gender, *Globalisation, Societies and Education* Vol 9 no 2 p 183–209

Laudel, G. 2005. Migration currents among the scientific elite. *Minerva*, Vol. 43, No. 4.

Ministry of Education, Education Strategic Plan 2012–2016

Leemann R J, Gender inequalities in transnational academic mobility and the ideal type of academic entrepreneur *Discourse: Studies in the Cultural Politics of Education* Vol 31 no 5 p 609_625

Mabukela, R & Magubane Z . 2004. Hear Our voices. Race, Gender and the Status of Black South African Women in the Academy. University of South Africa Press. Pretoria.

Mamdani, M. 2007. Scholars in the marketplace: The dilemmas of neo-liberal reform at Makerere University 1989–2005. Council for development of social science research in Africa (CODESRIA), Dakar..

Mario, M, P. Fry And L. Leve. 2003. *Higher Education in Mozambique. Partnership for higher education in Africa.* James Currey and UEM, Oxford and Maputo.

MORE. 2010. Study on the mobility patterns and career paths of EU researchers. Final report (deliverable 7), prepared for the Commission Research Directorate C – European Research Area Universities and Researchers.

Morley L 1999. Organising Feminisms. The Micropolitics of the Academy. Macmillan press.

Morley L. 2005. Gender Equity in commonwealth Higher Education. Women Studies International Forum Issue. 28. pp. 209–221.

Morley L. 2006. Hidden transcripts: The micropolitics of gender in commonwealth Universities. Women Studies International Forum Issue. 29 pp 543–551.

Mozambique science, technology and innovation strategy (MOSTIS). 2006. Republic of Mozambique. Council of Ministers.

Mungazi, D. and L.K.Walker. Educational reform and the transformation of southern Africa.

Mählck, P. 2013. Academic Women in the global knowledge economy: Bodies, hierarchies and resistance. *Women's Studies International Forum*, Vol. 36, pp. 65–74.

Mählck, P. (2012), Forskningsprofiliering, differentiering och excellens: Om kön, tystnad och performativa vithetshandlingar. [Research profiling, differentiation and excellence: intersectional perspectives of gender inequality in the new research landscape], Tidskrift för Genusvetenskap nr 1–2.

Mählck, P. and B. Thaver. 2010. Dialogue on Gender and Race Equality. Conversations between Sweden and South Africa. *Equality, diversity and inclusion. An international Journal* (formerly Equal Opportunities International), Vol. 29, No. 1, pp. 23–37.

Mählck, P. 2003/2008. *Mapping Gender in Academic Workplaces. Ways of reproducing gender inequality within the discourse of Equality.* VDM Verlag, Saarbrucken, Germany

National Science Foundation, Division of Science Resources Statistics. 2003. *Gender Differences in the Careers of Academic Scientists and Engineers: A Literature Review.* NSF 03–322, Project Officer, Alan I. Rappoport. ArlingtonVA.

National Statistical Institute: Statistical yearbook 2012

Newitt, M. [date?]. *A History of Mozambique.* [Publisher? Place?]

OECD. 2012. Fact book 2011–2012: Economic, environmental and social statistics. OECD, Paris.

OECD. 2007. Mapping careers and mobility of doctoral holders: Draft guidelines, model questionnaire and indicators. STI working paper. OECD, Paris.

OECD. 2002. Proposed standard practice for surveys on research and experimental development: Frascati manual. OECD, Paris.

OECD. 1995. The measurement of scientific and technological activities: Manual on the measurement of human resources devoted to S&T: Canberra Manual. OECD, Paris.

Samoff, J. and B. Carrol. 2004. Conditions, coalitions and influence: The World Bank and higher education in Africa. Paper prepared for the annual conference of Comparative and International Education Society, Salt Lake City, 8–12 March. Stanford University.

Sida. 2009. Tracing research capacities in Viet Nam: Perspectives from Vietnamese researchers, Viet Nam – Swedish research cooperation. Sida secretariat for research cooperation, Stockholm.

Sida. 2006. Sida/SAREC bilateral research cooperation: Lessons learned. Sida Evaluation 06/17. Department for Evaluation of Internal Audit.

Sida. 2003. Sida support to the University Eduardo Mondlane, Mozambique. Sida Evaluation 03/35. Department for Research Co-operation.

Swedish Government. 2010. Research for development: Policy for research in Swedish development cooperation 2010–2014 and strategy for Sida's support for research cooperation 2010 –2014. Swedish Government Offices.

Teferra, D. And H. Greijn (eds). 2010. *Higher education and globalization: Challenges, threats and opportunities for Africa.* Maastricht University, Maastricht.

Teferre, D and Altbach, P. 2004. African higher education: Challenges for the 21st century. Higher Education, Vil 47, Issue 1, p 21–50.

Thaver, B. and P. Mählck. 2010. Diversity transactions in the academic profession: Reflections on Sweden and South Africa. *South African Review of Sociology*, Vol, 40, No. 1.

Thomas, K. 1990. *Gender and Subject in Higher Education.* Open University Press, Milton Keynes.

Thorbecke, E. 2013. The interrelationship linking growth, inequality and poverty in sub-Saharan Africa. *Journal of African Economics*, Vol. 22, Supplement 1, pp. [??].

Toutkoushian, R. 1999. The status of women in academe in the 1990s. No longer outsiders but not yet equals. *Quarterly Review of Economics and Finance*, Vol. 39, pp. 679–98.

Tremblay, K. 2009. Academic mobility and immigration. Journal of Studies in International Education, Vol. 9, Issue [??], pp. [??].

UNDP. 2013. Human Development Report 2013: The rice of the south; human progress in a diverse world. UNDP, New York.

UNESCO. 2010. UNESCO Science Report: The current status of science around the world. UNESCO, Paris.

UNESCO. 2006. Global education digest 2006. UNESCO Publishing, Montreal.

Unhalter. E. 2006. New times and new vocabularies: Theorising and evaluating gender equality in Commonwealth higher Education. *Women Studies International Forum, Vol.* 29, Issue [??], pp. 620–8.

Varghese, N. 2004. Private higher education in Africa. International Institute for Educational Planning (IIEP). UNESCO, Geneva.

World Bank. 1988. Education in Sub-Saharan Africa: strategies for adjustment, revitalisation and expansion. World Bank, Washington DC.

Zuckerman, H. 1991. The careers of men and Women scientists. A review of current research. In H. Zuckerman, *J. Cole* and J. Bruer (eds), *The Outer Circle: Women in the Scientific Community*. Norton, New York.

Appendix

Appendix I: Methodology

Sample

The questionnaire was sent to all 159 traced individuals. The response rate was 51.6 per cent (82 individuals). Of the respondents, 56.1 per cent hold a PhD (46 individuals in total, 31 with degrees from Sweden and 15 with degrees from South Africa) and 43.9 per cent are in training (36 individuals, 18 each in training in Sweden and in South Africa). This is a comparatively good response rate.[44] In total, 20 interviews were conducted and analysed. For this group of researchers, we have striven for maximum variation in gender, age, discipline and year of graduation. Seven women and 13 men were interviewed. The positions held were lecturer, head of department, head of NGO, dean, vice rector and senior policy advisor.

Table: 1.1 Total sampled population by country of graduation/training, discipline and gender

| | Sweden | | | | | | | | | | | | South Africa | | | | | | | | | | | | Tot |
| | Med | | Sci | | Soc | | Vet | | Tech | | Agri | | Med | | Sci | | Soc | | Vet | | Tech | | Agri | | |
	F	M	F	M	F	M	F	M	F	M	F	M	F	M	F	M	F	M	F	M	F	M	F	M	F/M
Graduated	9	1	1	12	3	1	1	1	1	12	0	3	0	0	0	14	3	1	0	2	0	0	0	0	65
In training	9	8	12	24	4	2	0	0	0	3	0	7	0	0	2	7	6	1	3	1	0	3	0	2	94
Total	18	9	13	36	7	3	1	1	1	15	0	10	0	0	2	21	9	2	3	3	0	3	0	2	159

Drop-outs (5 in total, 4 in medicine and one in agricultural science) are excluded.

Method

The survey and interviews have been analysed using a multi-methods approach (Allwood 2004). This means different perspectives on research careers and mobility can be discussed and/or combined and integrated (Allwood 2004). The survey has been designed and coded with the help of Artologik web-based software.[45] In terms of representation of certain categories, the response rate has also been fairly high, particularly in the categories important to this study – gender, age, discipline, country of graduation/training and year of graduation. Thus, no weighting calculations of any categories of respondent have been made. The survey was organised around themes such as 1) the PhD student's dates; 2) academic career and mobility after graduation with PhD; and 3) current research situation in Mozambique. Consequently, a large overview of tendencies within the group has been produced.

---

44. The response rate for similar studies of European PhD graduates has been much lower, and was 11 per cent in the MORE project.
45. Artologik survey and report is software for the construction and operation of web-based surveys.

Individual interviews were semi-structured around themes related to the survey, but also emphasised personal experience of mobility and/or stickiness, structures of inequality related to gender, age, academic discipline and context specific experiences of discrimination based on skin-colour and nationality. The interviews lasted on average between one and two hours (see appendix for interview guide and letter of agreement). Most interviews were recorded and crucial sections have been transcribed. Interviews were also conducted with staff in strategic positions in the university administration and in relevant government bodies. Following the intersectional research design, tensions and contradictions between differently situated researchers were particularly analysed. Attention was also given to tensions between the tendencies produced by large-scale mapping as compared to the nuances highlighted in the personal narratives during interviews.

Limitations

The study does not particularly explore recruitment processes for PhD training programs. This does not mean this is not an important aspect of the production and reproduction of research capacity. On the contrary, we suggest this topic would require a different research design that would require a longer period of fieldwork in order to gain the full archival access needed to trace researchers who applied but were not accepted, as well as to build the alliances and trust necessary to explore the possible functioning/non-functioning of the academic reward system.

It is also worth noting that we only focused on researchers who participated in the Sida-funded program for research cooperation. Researchers who participated in other donor-supported PhD training programs have not been included.

Appendix II: Web-based questionnaire

Survey on mobility and career paths of Ph.D. holders in the Swedish research cooperation with Mozambique

Information about the survey

This study is conduced by the Nordic Africa Institute, Uppsala, Sweden and financed by the Embassy of Sweden, Maputo, Mozambique.

This questionnaire is part of a project conducted by the Nordic Africa Institute in Uppsala, Sweden on mobility and career paths of donor supported Ph.D. holders in Africa. The overall objective of the project is to longitudinally and comparatively map and analyse modes and rationales behind mobility and career paths/choices among Ph.D. holders in different academic disciplines funded within the frames of different donor's support to institutional research capacity building in Africa. The project will primarily investigate the extent and direction of geographic and sectorial mobility over time and perceptions and individual rationales behind mobility and career choices. An important part of the project is also to investigate experiences made from participating in Ph.D. training programs.

The main objectives of the questionnaire are:

- to collect internationally comparable data on the careers of holders of advanced research qualifications.

- to establish and analyse trends in the career paths and mobility of highly qualified people in Africa.

This survey is specifically designed for the Ph.D. holders that have been trained within the frame of the Swedish research cooperation with Mozambique. The survey covers all Ph.D. holders that have graduated between 1980 and 2012.

In this survey we will ask you questions about your participation in the Sida funded Ph.D. training program and your mobility and career paths since graduation.

Any information publicly released (such as statistical summaries) will be in a form that does not personally identify you.

Your response is voluntary and failure to provide some or all of the requested information will not in any way adversely affect you.

Actual time to complete the questionnaire may vary depending on your circumstances. On average, it will take about 10- 20 minutes to complete the questionnaire.

Your assistance is essential to ensure that the results are meaningful. Your answers will be kept strictly confidential and used for statistical purposes only.

The findings of the study will help the stakeholders involved in the research cooperation (Government of Mozambique, Swedish development actors and universities) to set up appropriate policies with regard to highly qualified people in order to ensure their career developments and to improve development support to research training.

For further information about the project please visit the web site www.nai.se or contact the project leader Måns Fellesson - mans.fellesson@nai.uu.se

Thank you very much for your time and collaboration

Måns Fellesson & Paula Mählck

The Nordic Africa Institute
Box 1703, 751 47 Uppsala, Sweden
Phone: +46 18 471 52 00
Fax: +46 18 56 22 90
E-mail: nai@nai.uu.se

Module I : Socio-demographics

1. Gender

○ Female

○ Male

2. Year of birth

3. Country of birth

4. Country of residence

5. Country or countries of citizenship

6. Marital status

☐ Married

☐ Single

☐ Divorced

☐ Widowed

☐ Partner

☐ Other

7. Do you have children?

○ Yes

○ No

8. If yes on question 7, how many?

☐ 1

☐ 2

☐ 3

☐ 4

☐ 5 and more

9. If yes on question 7, how old is your youngest child?

☐ 0 - 5

☐ 6 - 10

☐ 11 - 15

☐ 16- 20

☐ 21 -

10. If yes on question 7, how old is your oldest child?

☐ 0 -5

☐ 6 - 10

☐ 11 - 15

☐ 16 - 20

☐ 21 -

Module II : Educational attainment

11. Year of starting Ph.D. training

[ ]

12. Year of graduation Ph.D. degree

[ ]

13. Country of graduation Ph.D. degree

[ ]

14. Discipline of science Ph.D. degree

☐ Social science

☐ Science

☐ Medicine

☐ Humanities

☐ Technology

☐ Agricultural science

15. Year of master degree or equivalent

[ ]

16. Discipline of science master degree

☐ Social science

☐ Science

☐ Medicine

☐ Humanities

☐ Technology

☐ Agricultural science

Module III : The period of Ph.D. training

17. Was your Ph.D. training organized in accordance with the "Sandwich" model?

◯ Yes

◯ No, please specify how it was organized

```

```

18. Which university did you belong to before starting your Ph.D. training?

☐ Eduardo Mondlane University

☐ Other university, please specify

```

```

19. In what country did you graduate (Ph.D. level)?

☐ In Sweden

☐ In South Africa

☐ In another country, please specify country and university

```

```

20. If graduated in Sweden please specify cooperation university and department in Sweden

```

```

21. If graduated in South Africa please specify cooperation university and department in South Africa

```

```

22. What type of dissertation did you write?

☐ Dissertation by monograph

☐ Dissertation by articles

23. What was your position at the time of starting the Ph.D. training

☐ Post-graduate student

☐ Staff member

☐ Other. Please specify

24. If graduating in Sweden, how many months in total did you spend in Sweden during your period of Ph.D. training?

☐ 0 - 6 months

☐ 7 - 13 months

☐ 14 - 19 months

☐ 20 - 26 months

☐ More than 26 months

25. If graduating in South Africa, how many months in total did you spend in Sweden during your period of Ph.D. training?

☐ 0 - 6 months

☐ 7 - 13 months

☐ 14 - 19 months

☐ 20 - 26 months

☐ More than 26 months

26. What was the average number of months each stay?

☐ 2 - 3 months

☐ 4 - 5 months

☐ 6 - 7 months

☐ 8 - 9 months

☐ 10 - 11 months

☐ 12 -

27. How did you experience the period of training in relation to the following aspects?

	Mostly very good	Mostly good	Mostly difficult	Mostly very difficult
Period of research training while at the host university in Sweden/South Africa	O	O	O	O
Period of research training while at the home university in Mozambique	O	O	O	O
Supervision in Sweden/South Africa	O	O	O	O
Co-supervision in Mozambuque	O	O	O	O
Resources (equipment and time) for research at the host university in Sweden/South Africa	O	O	O	O
Resources (equipment and time) for research at the home university in Mozambique	O	O	O	O

28. To what extent have you during the time of Ph.D. training while in Sweden/South Africa experienced discrimination ranging from unwanted attention to direct harassment on the basis of the following?

	To a very large extent	To a large extent	To a small extent	To a very small extent	Not at all
Gender	O	O	O	O	O
Age	O	O	O	O	O
Ethnic background	O	O	O	O	O
Socio-economic background (class)	O	O	O	O	O
Color of skin	O	O	O	O	O
Sexual orientation	O	O	O	O	O
Disability	O	O	O	O	O
Position at the workplace	O	O	O	O	O
Family situation (caring responsibility children, parents, etc)	O	O	O	O	O

29. To what extent have you during the time of Ph.D. training while at your home university in Mozambique experienced discrimination ranging from unwanted attention to direct harassment on the basis of the following?

	To a very large extent	To a large extent	To a small extent	To a very small extent	Not at all
Gender	○	○	○	○	○
Age	○	○	○	○	○
Ethnic background	○	○	○	○	○
Socio-economic background (class)	○	○	○	○	○
Color of skin	○	○	○	○	○
Sexual orientation	○	○	○	○	○
Disability	○	○	○	○	○
Position at the workplace	○	○	○	○	○
Family situation (caring responsibility children, parents, etc)	○	○	○	○	○

30. Describe in short, what did you experience as being the most positive features of the "sandwich" model?

31. Describe in short, what did you experience as being the most negative features of the "sandwich" model?

32. At present, do you have any contact with the collaborating (Ph.D. graduating) department in Sweden, South Africa or elsewhere?

○ Yes

○ No

33. if yes, what type of contact?

☐ Research cooperation, joint research project

☐ Lecturing

☐ Supervision of Ph.D. candidate

☐ Administrative collaboration

☐ Other, please specify

Module IV : Employments/positions since graduation - sectorial mobility

34. Where is your current principal employment/position?

☐ Eduardo Mondlane University

☐ Other university in Mozambique. Please specify below which university

☐ Other university outside Mozambique. Please specify below which country and university

☐ Other government/public agency/organization/actor in Mozambique. Please specify below which agency/organization/actor

☐ Private sector company/organization/actor in Mozambique. Please specify below which agency/organization/actor

☐ International donor/aid organizations/ NGOs in Mozambique. Please specify below which organization/NGO

☐ Other government/public agency/organization/actor outside Mozambique. Please specify below which country and agency/organization/actor

☐ Private sector company/organization/actor outside Mozambique. Please specify below which country and agency/organization/actor

☐ International donor organizations/ NGOs outside Mozambique. Please specify which country and organization/NGO

☐ Self-employed. Own business/consultant

☐ Unemployed

☐ Other. Please specify

Specify:

35. Do you currently have more than one income generating employment/job/activity?

○ Yes. Specify below how many and what type

○ No

```
┌─────────────────────────────────────────────────────────────┐
│                                                               │
│                                                               │
│                                                               │
└─────────────────────────────────────────────────────────────┘
```

36. What is your current position?

☐ Executive (minister, director general, etc)

☐ Professor

☐ Associate professor

☐ Head of department

☐ Lecturer

☐ Professional staff (medical doctor, agronomist, forester, etc)

☐ High official/official government organization, international organization, NGO

☐ Senior management, middle management (private sector)

☐ Consultant

☐ Other, please specify

```
┌─────────────────────────────────────────────────────────────┐
│                                                               │
│                                                               │
│                                                               │
└─────────────────────────────────────────────────────────────┘
```

37. Are you working on research with researchers in a country other than the one you are living in any of the following ways?

	Yes	No
Working on a joint publication with people in another country	○	○
Collaborating at a distance on a joint research project with researchers in another country	○	○
Fund raising collaboration, joint applications	○	○

38. If you have collaboration with researchers in other countries, which region does it mainly concern?

☐ Africa

☐ Europe

☐ North America

☐ Latin America

☐ Asia

Module VI : Working conditions

39. To what extent has your Ph.D. degree contributed to your current position?

Very much	Much	Little	Very little
○	○	○	○

40. To what extent do your current work tasks correspond to your academic qualifications?

To a very large extent	To a large extent	To a small extent	To a very small extent	Not at all
○	○	○	○	○

41. If low degree of correspondence, please indicate if you feel over-qualified or under-qualified

☐ Over-qualified

☐ Under-qualified

42. Please rate your satisfaction with your current position

	Very satisfied	Satisfied	Dissatisfied	Very dissatisfied
Salary	○	○	○	○
Working conditions	○	○	○	○
Job security	○	○	○	○
Opportunities for career advancement	○	○	○	○
Intellectual challenge	○	○	○	○
Level of responsibility	○	○	○	○
Degree of independence	○	○	○	○
Contribution to society	○	○	○	○

Social status	O	O	O	O
Overall level of satisfaction	O	O	O	O

43. To what extent have you from time of graduation up to your current position experienced discrimination ranging from unwanted attention to direct harassment on the basis of the following?

	To a very large extent	To a large extent	To a small extent	To a very small extent	Not at all
Gender	O	O	O	O	O
Age	O	O	O	O	O
Ethnic background	O	O	O	O	O
Socio-economic background (class)	O	O	O	O	O
Color of skin	O	O	O	O	O
Sexual orientation	O	O	O	O	O
Disability	O	O	O	O	O
Position at the workplace	O	O	O	O	O
Family situation (caring responsibility children, parents, etc)	O	O	O	O	O

44. Besides your current position, how many employment/positions have you held since graduation?

- ☐ 1 - 2 positions
- ☐ 3 - 4 positions
- ☐ 5 - 6 positions
- ☐ 7 - 8 positions
- ☐ 9 - 10 positions
- ☐ More than 10 positions

45. How many employments/positions at an university as researcher/teacher/administrator

- ☐ 1 - 2 positions
- ☐ 3 - 4 positions
- ☐ 5 - 6 positions
- ☐ 7 - 8 positions
- ☐ 9 -10 positions

☐ More than 10 positions

46. If you have had employments/positions outside the university, what type? The selection of multiple options is possible

☐ Other government/public agency/organization/actor in Mozambique. Please specify below which agency/organization/actor

☐ Private sector company/organization/actor in Mozambique. Please specify below which agency/organization/actor

☐ International donor/aid organizations/ NGOs in Mozambique. Please specify below which organization/NGO

☐ Other government/public agency/organization/actor outside Mozambique. Please specify below which country and agency/organization/actor

☐ Private sector company/organization/actor outside Mozambique. Please specify below which country and agency/organization/actor

☐ International donor organizations/ NGOs outside Mozambique. Please specify which country and organization/NGO

☐ Self-employed. Own business/consultant

☐ Other. Please specify

Specify:

Module V : Employments/positions since graduation - geographic mobility

47. Have you ever worked abroad since graduation?

○ Yes
○ No

48. if yes, please provide the name(s) of the country (countries) and duration of stay for each country

49. What kind of work/positions did you have during your stay(s) abroad? Several options possible

- ☐ Researcher
- ☐ Lecturer
- ☐ Official (government, international organization, NGO)
- ☐ Employee in the private sector
- ☐ Consultant
- ☐ Other, please specify

---

50. How important have the following aspects been for your decisions to work abroad?

	Very important	Important	Minor importance	Not important at all
Working conditions/facilities for research	○	○	○	○
Salary	○	○	○	○
Career development	○	○	○	○
Language/culture	○	○	○	○
Recognition of educational degrees	○	○	○	○
The existence of leading experts in your field	○	○	○	○
Existence of alternative employments	○	○	○	○
Development opportunities for family members (schools, employment, etc)	○	○	○	○

Other important aspects:

---

51. If you have a position at an university, to what extent do you conduct research?

Full-time	75 % of full-time	50 % of full-time	25 % of full-time	Less than 25 % of full-time	No at all
○	○	○	○	○	○

52. If you conduct research, how is it financed?

☐ The government (Mozambique)

☐ International donor

☐ International research funding (foundations)

☐ Private funding (business, industry)

☐ Other, please specify

53. If you conduct research to what extent have you, since graduation, published your research results in the following types of publications?

	To a large extent	To some extent	To a small extent	Not at all
Peer-reviewed international journals	○	○	○	○
Peer-reviewed national journals	○	○	○	○
University reports	○	○	○	○
Other reports (government/international organizations, NGOs, private sector)	○	○	○	○
Books	○	○	○	○
Teaching material	○	○	○	○
Papers for seminars/conferences/workshops	○	○	○	○

54. To what extent are you involved in following types of research network?

	To large extent	To some extent	To a small extent	Not at all
International (global) research networks involving researchers from many countries	○	○	○	○
Pan-African or regional research networks involving researchers from African countries	○	○	○	○
National research				

networks involving
researchers from
Mozambiquan research
institutions

  ○   ○   ○   ○

55. If you have a position at an university, to what extent are you involved in coursework lecturing?

Full-time	75 % of full-time	50 % of full-time	25 % of full-time	Less than 25 % of full-time	No at all
○	○	○	○	○	○

56. Do what extent do think your research results have contributed to the following ?

	To large extent	To some extent	To a small extent	Not at all
Policy development (government)	○	○	○	○
Poverty reduction in Mozambique	○	○	○	○
Advancement of the international research frontline	○	○	○	○
Advancement of the national research frontline	○	○	○	○

57. How many publications of the following types have you had since graduation?

	No publications	1 - 3	4 - 6	7 - 9	10 - 12	13 or more
Peer-reviewed international journals	○	○	○	○	○	○
Peer-reviewed national journals	○	○	○	○	○	○
University reports (non peer-reviewed)	○	○	○	○	○	○
Books	○	○	○	○	○	○
Papers for seminars/conferences/workshops	○	○	○	○	○	○

Module VII : Future plans

58. If picture yourself three years from now, to what extent do thing you are doing the following?

	Most likely	Possibly	Not likely	Don't know
Work at the Eduardo Mondlane University as a researcher	O	O	O	O
Work at the Eduardo Mondlane University as a lecturer	O	O	O	O
Work at another university/university collage in Mozambique	O	O	O	O
Work at an university/research institution in another country in the region	O	O	O	O
Work at an university/research institution in another country outside Africa	O	O	O	O
Work for a government agency in Mozambique	O	O	O	O
Work for an international organization/NGO in Mozambique	O	O	O	O
Work for an international organization/NGO abroad	O	O	O	O
Work for a private business company in Mozambique	O	O	O	O
Work for a private business company abroad	O	O	O	O
Having my own business (consult)	O	O	O	O

59. Would you be interested in positions at universities or other employments abroad?

O Yes

O No

60. If yes, how do you rate the importance of the following potential obstacles for mobility?

	Very important factor	Important factor	Not so important factor	Not important at all
Lack of employment opportunities	O	O	O	O
Language limitations	O	O	O	O
Family situation	O	O	O	O
Risk of discrimination (gender, age, ethnic and social background, skin color, disability, sexual orientation)	O	O	O	O

Many thanks for your participation
Please do not forget to send back the questionnaire

Appendix III: Interview guide

Mobility and careers paths among Ph.D. holders in the Swedish research collaboration with Mozambique 1990 – 2012

Module I: Socio-demographics
Background:
Age
Parents' occupation and self-categorisation of class background.
Marital status
Children, how many and year of birth
Country of residence, country of citizenship
Self-categorisation of ethnicity and race

Module II: Educational attainment
Year of entering PhD training
Year of PhD examination
Country of graduation of PhD

Module IV and V: Employment/ positions since graduation – sectoral and geographic mobility
Where/what is your current employment/position? How did you get your current position?
Do you have more than one employment/position or income generating activity?
Can you describe your journey from graduation to your position today; does it include mobility (sectoral, geographic, vertical)?
What as been the incentives/motivations for your career choices? What have been most difficult, easy/rewarding with your career development?
What have been hindering/impeding factors for your career development – foremost related to mobility?
To what extent and in what way has your Ph.D. degree contributed to your current position?
Do your current work tasks correspond to your academic qualification?
Has your research work been cited or used in any other ways in your country of residence, how?
What kind of networks do you currently have? (Types, regions)
Do you have any contacts with the collaborating department/researchers in Sweden? What kind of contact– network, etc. and what have it meant for your career development?

Module VI: Development of research and higher education

How do you view the current development of research and higher education in Mozambique? (Development, policy priorities and challenges) Can you describe research policy priorities in terms of basic research and applied research? What about commodification of research in policy and practice? What is the effect on research capacity building and aspects of equality such as gender?

Can you describe the horizon of internationalization in Mozambique? (Relation to other countries and regions, types of relations)

In what ways have the development of research and higher education in Mozambique influenced your career development?

Module III: The period of PhD training

What do you think are the advantages/disadvantages with the "sandwich" model?

Can you describe the recruitment process? (Process of selection, information, discrimination)

Which university and department in Sweden/South Africa were you affiliated to?

What was your research topic, how come you ended up with this topic? Could choose your supervisors? To what extent could you influence these processes?

How often did you go to Sweden/ South Africa?

What have been most difficult, easy/rewarding with your Ph.D. training?

How did you experience your staying in Sweden/ South Africa in terms of:

- The administrative arrangements? (Booking travels, housing, salaries, access to university facilities, visa procedures)
- The scientific rewards (development for your PhD training ie thesis and courses)
- Social relations i.e. integration in formal and informal networks and research collaborations at the Swedish/ South African department
- How did you organise your family life during this period? Did your family life change during this period, how?
- Can you describe what emotions/feelings are attached to this period of your life?

Did your relationship to your colleagues and your position at the department in your country of residence change as consequence of entering Ph.D. training? How?

Have you experienced negative treatment during your PhD training in Sweden/ South Africa and/or at your home university in terms of harassment or subtle discrimination based on your sexuality, gender, age, social class background, ethnicity or skin colour? Please describe.

Do you think your experiences of the previous question would have been different if you have had another gender, sexuality, age, class background, ethnicity or skin colour?

Within the program, what social attributes were associated with a good researcher? Did it differ between the department in Sweden/South Africa and in your home university? Have the features changed over time?

Can you visualise a good researcher?

Module VII: Future plans

What are your future plans? (mobility and career development)

Would you like to ask me something, about the study or any of the questions, make any adjustments to the answers?

Appendix IV: Ethical information to the respondents

Study on mobility and career paths of Ph.D. holders in the Swedish Research cooperation with Mozambique

Ethical information about the project

This study is conduced by the Nordic Africa Institute, Uppsala, Sweden and financed by the Embassy of Sweden, Maputo, Mozambique.

The study is part of a project conducted by the Nordic Africa Institute in Uppsala, Sweden on mobility and career paths of donor supported Ph.D. holders in Africa. The overall objective of the project is to longitudinally and comparatively map and analyse modes and rationales behind mobility and career paths/choices among Ph.D. holders in different academic disciplines funded within the frames of different donor's support to institutional research capacity building in Africa. The project will primarily investigate the extent and direction of geographic and sectoral mobility over time and perceptions and individual rationales behind mobility and career choices. An important part of the project is also to investigate experiences made from participating in Ph.D. training programs.

The project has been ethically tested and approved by the Central Ethical Review Board in Uppsala, Sweden. The project is done in accordance to the regulations of Swedish ethics in research.

Your answers will be kept strictly confidential and used for research purposes only.

Any information publicly released (such as statistical summaries or quotes) will be in a form that does not personally identify you.

Your response is voluntary and failure to provide some or all of the requested information will not in any way adversely affect you.

You can at any time choose to discontinue the interview.

For further information about the project please visit the web site www.nai.se or contact the project leader Måns Fellesson – mans.fellesson@nai.uu.se

The Nordic Africa Institute

Box 1703, 751 47 Uppsala, Sweden
Phone: +46 18 471 52 00
Fax: +46 18 56 22 90
E-mail. nai@nai.uu.se

CURRENT AFRICAN ISSUES PUBLISHED BY THE INSTITUTE
Recent issues in the series are available electronically
for download free of charge www.nai.uu.se

1981

1. *South Africa, the West and the Frontline States. Report from a Seminar.*

2. Maja Naur, *Social and Organisational Change in Libya.*

3. *Peasants and Agricultural Production in Africa. A Nordic Research Seminar. Follow-up Reports and Discussions.*

1985

4. Ray Bush & S. Kibble, *Destabilisation in Southern Africa, an Overview.*

5. Bertil Egerö, *Mozambique and the Southern African Struggle for Liberation.*

1986

6. Carol B.Thompson, *Regional Economic Polic under Crisis Condition. Southern African Development.*

1989

7. Inge Tvedten, *The War in Angola, Internal Conditions for Peace and Recovery.*

8. Patrick Wilmot, *Nigeria's Southern Africa Policy 1960–1988.*

1990

9. Jonathan Baker, *Perestroika for Ethiopia: In Search of the End of the Rainbow?*

10. Horace Campbell, *The Siege of Cuito Cuanavale.*

1991

11. Maria Bongartz, *The Civil War in Somalia. Its genesis and dynamics.*

12. Shadrack B.O. Gutto, *Human and People's Rights in Africa. Myths, Realities and Prospects.*

13. Said Chikhi, Algeria. *From Mass Rebellion to Workers' Protest.*

14. Bertil Odén, *Namibia's Economic Links to South Africa.*

1992

15. Cervenka Zdenek, *African National Congress Meets Eastern Europe. A Dialogue on Common Experiences.*

1993

16. Diallo Garba, *Mauritania–The Other Apartheid?*

1994

17. Zdenek Cervenka and Colin Legum, *Can National Dialogue Break the Power of Terror in Burundi?*

18. Erik Nordberg and Uno Winblad, *Urban Environmental Health and Hygiene in Sub-Saharan Africa.*

1996

19. Chris Dunton and Mai Palmberg, *Human Rights and Homosexuality in Southern Africa.*

1998

20. Georges Nzongola-Ntalaja, *From Zaire to the Democratic Republic of the Congo.*

1999

21. Filip Reyntjens, *Talking or Fighting? Political Evolution in Rwanda and Burundi, 1998–1999.*

22. Herbert Weiss, *War and Peace in the Democratic Republic of the Congo.*

2000

23. Filip Reyntjens, *Small States in an Unstable Region – Rwanda and Burundi, 1999–2000.*

2001

24. Filip Reyntjens, *Again at the Crossroads: Rwanda and Burundi, 2000–2001.*

25. Henning Melber, *The New African Initiative and the African Union. A Preliminary Assessment and Documentation.*

2003

26. Dahilon Yassin Mohamoda, *Nile Basin Cooperation. A Review of the Literature.*

2004

27. Henning Melber (ed.), *Media, Public Discourse and Political Contestation in Zimbabwe.*

28. Georges Nzongola-Ntalaja, *From Zaire to the Democratic Republic of the Congo.* (Second and Revised Edition)

2005

29. Henning Melber (ed.), *Trade, Development, Cooperation – What Future for Africa?*

30. Kaniye S.A. Ebeku, *The Succession of Faure Gnassingbe to the Togolese Presidency – An International Law Perspective.*

31. J.V. Lazarus, C. Christiansen, L. Rosendal Østergaard, L.A. Richey, Models for Life – Advancing antiretroviral therapy in sub-Saharan Africa.

2006

32. Charles Manga Fombad & Zein Kebonang, *AU, NEPAD and the APRM – Democratisation Efforts Explored.* (Ed. H. Melber.)

33. P.P. Leite, C. Olsson, M. Schöldtz, T. Shelley, P. Wrange, H. Corell and K. Scheele, *The Western Sahara Conflict – The Role of Natural Resources in Decolonization.* (Ed. Claes Olsson)

2007

34. Jassey, Katja and Stella Nyanzi, *How to Be a "Proper" Woman in the Times of HIV and AIDS.*

35. M. Lee, H. Melber, S. Naidu and I. Taylor, *China in Africa.* (Compiled by Henning Melber)

36. Nathaniel King, *Conflict as Integration. Youth Aspiration to Personhood in the Teleology of Sierra Leone's 'Senseless War'.*

2008

37. Aderanti Adepoju, *Migration in sub-Saharan Africa.*

38. Bo Malmberg, *Demography and the development potential of sub-Saharan Africa.*

39. Johan Holmberg, *Natural resources in sub-Saharan Africa: Assets and vulnerabilities.*

40. Arne Bigsten and Dick Durevall, *The African economy and its role in the world economy.*

41. Fantu Cheru, *Africa's development in the 21st century: Reshaping the research agenda.*

2009

42. Dan Kuwali, *Persuasive Prevention. Towards a Principle for Implementing Article 4(h) and R2P by the African Union.*

43. Daniel Volman, *China, India, Russia and the United States. The Scramble for African Oil and the Militarization of the Continent.*

2010

44. Mats Hårsmar, *Understanding Poverty in Africa? A Navigation through Disputed Concepts, Data and Terrains.*

2011

45. Sam Maghimbi, Razack B. Lokina and Mathew A. Senga, *The Agrarian Question in Tanzania? A State of the Art Paper.*

46. William Minter, *African Migration, Global Inequalities, and Human Rights. Connecting the Dots.*

47. Musa Abutudu and Dauda Garuba, *Natural Resource Governance and EITI Implementation in Nigeria.*

48. Ilda Lindell, *Transnational Activism Networks and Gendered Gatekeeping. Negotiating Gender in an African Association of Informal Workers.*

2012

49. Terje Oestigaard, *Water Scarcity and Food Security along the Nile. Politics, population increase and climate change.*

50. David Ross Olanya, *From Global Land Grabbing for Biofuels to Acquisitions of AfricanWater for Commercial Agriculture.*

2013

51. Gessesse Dessie, *Favouring a Demonised Plant. Khat and Ethiopian smallholder enterprise.*

52. Boima Tucker, *Musical Violence. Gangsta Rap and Politics in Sierra Leone.*

53. David Nilsson, *Sweden-Norway at the Berlin Conference 1884–85. History, national identity-making and Sweden's relations with Africa.*

54. Pamela K. Mbabazi, *The Oil Industry in Uganda; A Blessing in Disquise or an all Too Familiar Curse? Paper presented at the Claude Ake Memorial Lecture.*

55. Måns Fellesson & Paula Mählck, *Academics on the Move. Mobility and Institutional Change in the Swedish Development Support to Research Capacity Buildiing in Mozambique.*

www.ingramcontent.com/pod-product-compliance
Lightning Source LLC
Chambersburg PA
CBHW080208300326
41934CB00038B/3410